P9-ASI-004

The Psychoaesthetic Experience

An Approach to Depth-Oriented Treatment

CONTRIBUTORS

David Read Johnson, Ph.D., R.D.T.
Department of Psychiatry
Yale University
New Haven, Connecticut
Veterans Administration Medical Center
West Haven, Connecticut

Priscilla Rodgers, M.P.S.
Psychoanalytic candidate
C. P. Jung Institute
New York, New York

Eileen Serlin, Ph.D.
Saybrook Institute, and private practice
San Francisco, California

Alice Shields, D.M.A.
Faculty, Rutgers University
New Brunswick, New Jersey
The New School for Social Research
New York, New York
Psychoanalytic candidate
Institute for Expressive Analysis
New York, New York
and private practice
New York, New York

The Psychoaesthetic Experience

An Approach to Depth-Oriented Treatment

Arthur Robbins, Ed.D., A.T.R.

Creative Arts Therapy Department
Pratt Institute
Brooklyn, New York
Institute for Expressive Analysis
New York, New York
and Faculty, National Psychological Association for Psychoanalysis
New York, New York

With contributions by
David Read Johnson, Ph.D., R.D.T.,
Priscilla Rodgers, M.P.S., Eileen Serlin, Ph.D.,
and Alice Shields, D.M.A.

Prepared in collaboration with colleagues of the
expressive therapy professions

 **HUMAN SCIENCES PRESS, INC.**

Library of Congress Cataloging in Publication Data

Robbins, Arthur, 1928–
    The psychoaesthetic experience: an approach to depth-oriented treatment / Arthur Robbins; prepared in collaboration with colleagues of the expressive therapy professions.
        p.   cm.
    Bibliography: p.
    Includes index.
    ISBN 0-89885-453-9
    1. Arts—Therapeutic use. I. Title.
RC489.A72R63   1989   88-17546
616.89'1656—dc19   CIP

© 1989 Human Sciences Press, Inc.
A Subsidiary of Plenum Publishing Corporation
233 Spring Street, New York, N.Y. 10013

Printed in the United States of America

Preface

I have just delivered a paper to the psychoanalytic society on the subject of the aesthetics of interpretation, and I am struck with the passion and conviction with which I spoke. For several years I have lectured and studied the parallels of the creative and therapeutic processes and more recently of the language and sensibilities of the artist that contribute to the science of psychoanalysis. Needless to say, there is a significant aspect of psychoanalytic treatment that involves clear, linear, and interpretive work, but there is also an indispensable level of nonverbal organization intrinsic to the treatment process that is governed by principles aesthetic in form, which constantly affects the pacing and patterning of verbal interpretations. Linear scientific terminology simply does not adequately describe the complexity of human relationships and inner life, and therefore cannot provide the "holding environment" most conducive to the exploration of these multi-fold areas.

The artist understands this complexity and comes much closer to expressing it in multidimensional symbolic forms. All of us undoubtedly have experienced this phenomenon at some time: while looking at a piece of artwork, listening to a musical passage, reading a poem, or seeing a dance; and though we felt a fullness of understanding of what it is to be human, we could not explain it verbally. The multidimensionality of the art form has captured a certain intricate "truth" that cannot be reduced to a monodimensional description. It stands to reason, then, that if we are to understand the true essence of and be maximally effective in this very complex interchange called psychoanalytic psychotherapy, we must explore and more consciously bind the two giants, art and science.

As is so often the case, when I think about the interface between psychoanalytic treatment and principles of aesthetics, I see an intertwining of my personal and professional selves that cannot easily be separated. I would therefore like to begin by offering a personal glimpse of my involvement in the dual worlds of art and science. The sculptor and psychologist inside me have not always lived easily with one another. In retrospect, I now smile at the image of myself playing in a sandbox as a young boy, altogether preoccupied with my secret hideaway of sandpiles, dark holes, and crevices. This was my bastion against the world. Indeed, this box *was* my world, for it was only there, steeped in sand, dirt, and water, that I felt I could be myself. My sandbox, however, was not confined to the back yard, for I would carry the "messages" of my world out to odd places in the house. In particular, I would find sinks and toilets in which to deposit my latest artistic creations, which of course made quite an impact upon my family—to say nothing of the plumbing bill! I continued to plug the various orifices in my house with my latest creations, feeling wonderment at the rage and distress of my parents. I didn't know then that this was the only way I was able to say to my family, as well as to myself, "I am; this is part of me." As much as my family worried aloud, and I, privately, about what would become of me, I continued to create my world in the present, preferring not to know about the neat, clean, orderly reality "out there."

I was surrounded by the world of aesthetics in my early years. My sister and mother would spend endless hours talking about the interior decoration of their house, for it was not my house, but theirs. Indeed, out of this intense preoccupation my sister developed a fine aesthetic sensibility and became an outstanding interior decorator in her adult life. My father, a manufacturer of artificial flowers, would constantly consult the women of the house regarding his newest creations and would receive their adulation or disapproval. These manifestations of the aesthetic seemed too beautiful, belonging to the world of my mother and sister and, to some degree, my father, but not to the dirty little boy in the sandbox. On the periphery of this scene were my father's siblings: two brothers and one sister were psychoanalysts. One of them, in fact, would be my supervisor when I attended an analytic institute. My mother was always somewhat suspicious of their occupation. It was her belief that *real* therapists were psychiatrists, not that other variety called lay analysts. They were, at best, shady and disreputable in her eyes. As I now reflect on my mother's attitude I wonder if it was indicative of her deep distrust of men—all men representing her abandoning father who left home when she was 2 years old. In consideration of my family history, therefore, it's no wonder I retreated to the sandbox!

So there I was immersed in my daily dirtiness, sometimes frightened by my phallic aspirations, worried about my messiness, and developing an identity of Arthur the "schlump." Fortunately, the family pattern was clear and obvious; not a small gift as I recall. This permitted me to take some distance as I grew up to become somewhat insulated from the intricacies of these dynamics. Having developed an avid interest in psychology at an early age, I was able to explore the uncomfortable dynamics of my family, and soon after receiving my doctorate, I entered an analytic institute. Freud articulated the language of my unconscious. He spoke to a deep part of myself—those secret passages in my soul—and gave me permission to look at the intricacies of sexuality.

Art, on the other hand, had become a symbol of fear and incompetence. I still recall in high school screaming in my sleep, "I don't want art, I can't handle it!" Art was altogether too enmeshed with the world of my mother. It was a place far too pretty and nice for me to handle. The deeper associations only became apparent during my analysis; yet, in spite of all my feeling to the contrary, I knew I had to return to the world of the sandbox. Seemingly out of nowhere, I made the decision to take a sculpting course after years of having been a therapist.

I'll never forget my first impressions of the sculpting room with its strange aroma that verged on the erotic. I remember peeking into the studio tentatively and hearing the busy sounds of artists at work. I was paralyzed by intense opposing feelings of excitement and fear. The teacher, an old, wise, Russian woman dressed in a long skirt and a blue apron, caught me in the act of peeking in, took one look at me, and bellowed, "Well, what are you waiting for?" Unable to run, I took my place at the table, only slowly looking out the corners of my eyes to see what was going on around me. My teacher directed me to a pot of clay and left me to my own resources. No one seemed too preoccupied with making anything beautiful or "nice," and reassured I started to play with this new material. My teacher seemed to know when to give me space, when I needed her help, always showing enjoyment at my creative endeavors. Slowly, I began a love affair with clay and the creative process, perhaps once again discovering the hidden order of my sandbox.

The material was at first delightfully challenging as I delved into my new playground to discover images and ideas that took shape as I worked the clay. I began to feel the rhythm of the clay, the texture, if not the very life-force of the material. Gradually, as I moved from clay to other media, I came to understand that aesthetics was the giving of life to the inanimate and the making of statements about who I was. I also became aware of the general parallels between the creative and therapeutic processes as well as the more specific crossover lessons between a particular medium and work with patients. Perhaps the first and most general observation I made in the studio was the realization that there was a rhythm to my creating, a moving in and out, as I'd first become one with the clay and then as I stepped back to observe shape and form. I noticed that this also applied to my work in my therapy office as I moved between joining with the patient to understand, empathize, and get a sense of resonance and then back out to organize, observe, and give form through verbalization.

Clay offered other lessons as well. For one thing, I started to consciously abstain from preforming or working out images or ideas until I put my hand to clay, thus leaving an openness to options. I attempted also to maintain this attitude with my patients by walking into the sessions without preconceptions or notions of what was going to happen. This was not always easy to maintain, and when I became anxious, I'd find myself preparing for a session in order to regain some measure of control over my therapeutic work. Sadly, this only diminished my ability to remain centered and aware of what my patients were experiencing at that moment.

In the course of letting images emerge in my work with clay, I was introduced to the wonderful world of symbolism. I quickly recognized an important tool for understanding both myself and my patients. I found that symbols became a codification—an organization of important parts of myself. Furthermore, I began to see how the deep spaces within myself could only be filled by personal symbols connecting a deep inner reality to the outside. One such symbol emerged in one of my first pieces: a child's conception of a sliding pond coming out of the image of a pregnant woman (Figure 1). I still take delight in thinking how wonderful it would be to slide down her belly. I also smile at the playfulness of

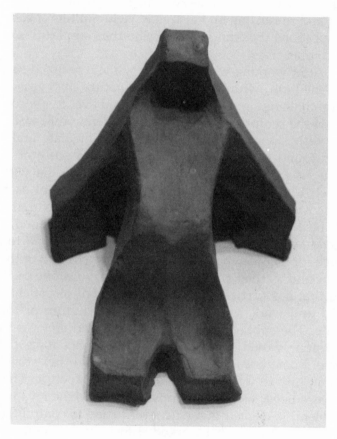

FIGURE 1

this image that pulls together a number of levels of meaning for me in a way that a verbal description could never have done. This marked the birth of my belief that the personal symbols and images of patients can be rich and rewarding and also may yield multilevel communications that can best describe the complexities of their inner lives.

After working with clay for a while, I realized that this medium, with its soft, pliable nature, had ceased to be challenging. One day, I wandered over to the corner of the sculpting studio where students were working with stone. My fascination was immediate and I soon found that the experience of being a sculptor of stone was quite different from the other media with which I had previously worked. The creation of each piece was perceived as similar to the experience of giving birth to a child, and as I grunted and moaned, I would swear I would never do it again. It was all too much for me. Slowly, I started to feel the rhythm of the stone and learned an important principle of stone carving that has carried over to my treatment of patients: Find and work with, not against, the rhythm of the stone. The subtle flow of indentations and crevices in the stone would point the way if I did not force the issue. Sometimes I'd engage in battle with my stone, attempting to force my will and control upon it. This process never yielded a happy solution to the creative problem. It seemed that whenever I tried to control the material with which I worked, I lost contact with the creative process. This has proved equally true in working with patients. I've learned that each patient–therapist relationship, like each piece of sculpture, has its own rhythm and if entered and joined, gives clues for directions which can then be utilized when one steps out of this oneness in order to evaluate the material. Indeed, there is a movement back and forth between being part of the material and then separating; in other words, an oscillation between formlessness and form, which defines the rhythm of the creative experience. If I fight the internal rhythm of a patient and try to impose my own rhythm, I run the danger of increasing resistance. From this experience a principle common to treatment became patently clear: Avoid a head-on collision with a major resistance.

A recent visit to a sculpture workshop reminded me of another lesson I had learned from my initial experience in stone sculpting. As I watched the students, many of whom were working with stone for the first time, some were unable to apply the appropriate force that was needed, seemingly out of fear that it was fragile and would break apart. (I have observed a similar fear in the therapists I supervise.) But it is important not to be afraid of the force one brings to the stone, knowing that it is only when one gets deeper into the work that one can really experience the nuances of resistance, energy, and curves, and therefore discover the most productive path. Likewise, as therapists we must immerse ourselves in the patient's material. We cannot stand apart and watch what is going on, nor can we be so afraid of our "therapeutic aggression" that we reject it as being dangerous or destructive.

My exploration of various sculpting materials eventually led to my work with metal. In working with this medium, I've always been most aware of the molten steel literally dancing before me. Here, it is important to harness the energy in "containers" that have positive and negative balances of space. Transferring this knowledge to the treatment process, I've moved in and out of my patients' therapeutic space, playing with polarities and searching out hidden opposites and valences. This looking for opposites reflects both a basic aesthetic principle and a truth about human character. People *are* complex mixtures of seeming contradictions, and images or metaphors have a way of capturing this "truth." If we as therapists understand the seeming contradictions or polarities in ourselves, we will be better able to help patients deal with their own. There is more, though: It is in fact the integrating of polarities into a greater whole that spells growth for all of us.

Often, as I've worked with symbols of sculpting, I've found myself dealing with the images of transition. One such image is that brought to mind by a piece I completed while teaching at the Summer Art Therapy Institute in Italy, where I had gone after teaching a summer program in New Hampshire. As I wandered around my new "home," a farm, I recalled my pleasure at discovering some old scraps of metal and, wonder of wonders, a welding machine. Having received permission to use the arc welder, I practiced maneuvering it for a while. Out of this experience came a very large metal piece that I have come to view as a symbol of transition (Figure 2). Unlike many of my creations, in it I detected an archetypal quality—one that seemed to connect many levels of consciousness and convey a meaning that was not bounded by any particular place: A part of me from New Hampshire had come along to say "hello" to my present environment. By creating this piece, I was able to connect the past to the present and synthesize and integrate pieces of my experience into a whole. As a result, I learned that images supersede any personal experience as they tap into the deep reservoir of symbols that goes beyond one's personal space; in-

FIGURE 2

deed, beyond the boundaries of a cultural matrix. My new-found knowledge of transition symbols and their function in integrating a piecemeal sense of self into a whole self has been an important part of my growth as an individual and as a therapist. For me, this has meant recognizing my tendency to compartmentalize the parts of my life in an effort to control anxiety, while through my patients I have seen how many people lack this concept of symbols, or symbols as a means of transition, and so are unable to connect their pasts, presents, and "other" levels of consciousness.

In all my sculpting, I've found that surprises and accidents provide wonderful inroads to new creations and forms. I've carried this notion into my work with patients, and rarely have found that an error could not be used in the service of a very creative and constructive interchange. It has been, indeed, these very errors or "problems" in treatment that have become the vehicles for reconstructive work, resculpting the past into new creative solutions for the present.

This text then, as can now be readily surmised, is a personal statement of the language of the artist as applied to depth-oriented therapy.

Science alone cannot open up the pathways for either patient or therapist to comprehend the complexity of subjective truth. The language of the artist has something special to offer the therapist in this regard and this text, hopefully, will make a contribution to interpreting how that "language" can be used effectively in the treatment process.

                                              Arthur Robbins

Berne, Switzerland

Acknowledgments

I owe a very special debt to my sculpting teacher, Lilly Ente, the arts therapy students at Pratt Institute, and the patients and supervisees with whom I have had the pleasure of working over the past 35 years of private practice. Each, in their unique and special way, has offered a very personal and intimate glimpse of the creative process in motion. I want to also thank Trudie Loubet and Priscilla Rodgers, both of whom have contributed to the overall editorial alignment of this text.

The following journals have generously permitted me to include in the text material that had originally appeared in these publications: Robbins, A. (1988), The interface of the real and transference relationship with schizoid phenomena. *The Psychoanalytic Review, 75,* 393–418, published by the National Psychological Association for Psychoanalysis, Inc., and Robbins, A. (1984), Interpretation as a means of organizing psychological space within the transference/countertransference relationship. *Modern Psychoanalysis, 9*, 7–14, published by the Center for Modern Psychoanalytic Studies.

Last, but not least, I want to thank my wife Sandy, for her confidence and support in this endeavor.

A.R.

Contents

1

Introduction:
The Psychoaesthetics of
Depth-Oriented Treatment

The relationship between psychoanalysis and art reads like a stormy love affair. I am reminded of Freud's (1928) famous statement: "Before the problem of the creative artist, analysis must, alas, lay down its arms." Freud, of course, never followed his famous dictum, but was clearly drawn to the mystery and magic of art. Yet, as a solitary pioneer fighting for the respectability of psychoanalysis as a science, the recognition of the aesthetics of psychoanalytic transference–countertransference communications was minimized. Indeed, from the various writings in the field, we are aware of the intrigue, ambivalence, and even disavowal of art.

The issues addressed in this chapter have been introduced in an article entitled: "A Psychoaesthetic Approach to Creative Arts Therapy Training" by Arthur Robbins, in the *Journal of Arts and Psychotherapy* (in print).

3

By contrast, Jung, in reacting to this cold, linear scientific approach, was receptive to artistic expression as an intrinsic part of the treatment process. He crossed the forbidden frontier in his efforts to incorporate Eastern mysticism into psychoanalytic theory, but even here, I suspect he tapped into the dark side of Freud. Yet for the most part, the early pioneers in psychoanalysis remained within Freud's perspective and viewed nonverbal expression as an inferior form of communication, placing enormous emphasis on verbal expression.

To this day, there are still psychoanalysts who remain within this framework, but as psychoanalysis has evolved in theory and practice, analysts have bridged the worlds of art and science. Less caught up in the need to maintain the respectability of psychoanalysis as a science, these theorists, in integrating art and science, have focused on one facet of treatment theory in particular: the realm of understanding the interface between the so-called "real" and transference relationships.

Mark Grunes (1984) offers an extensive overview of this literature and traces the range of positions that can be taken regarding this issue. For instance, he cites one group, including such therapists as Ferenczi and Balint, and later Alexander, who as clinicians conducted treatment within a working premise of an "emotional corrective experience." These therapists clearly stand in opposition to other analysts for whom the term "emotional corrective experience" remains an abhorrent one, being equated with the gratification of patients' infantile impulses and consequently a deterrent to reconstructive change. Grunes refers to other therapists, such as Greenson, who are less strict in dichotomizing the real and transferential relationships. Here, the humanity, consistency, discipline, and integrity of the analyst become important aspects of the treatment that permit the work of transference to proceed. Yet there is little question that the working through of resistance and transference is the central work of psychoanalytic treatment.

Grunes, inspired by the work of Loewald (1960), takes a further step in recognizing the influence of the real relationship that facilitates the interpretive work of treatment. If anything, he takes the position that the real and the transference relationships work hand-in-hand. The therapeutic style, therefore, of relating to one's patient is not viewed as gratifying infantile impulses but as a means to resonate and make contact with the patient. Thus, the analyst's ability to temporarily lessen personal boundaries and permit a permeability to exist between the patient and himself facilitates a symbolic relatedness that has been recognized as being particularly effective with patients exhibiting early pregenital developmental disorders. With this group of patients, the identification with the therapist is seen as a facilitator of object constancy. Working with this thesis, however, Grunes stops short of getting down to the nitty-gritty of enumerating or describing the aesthetic principles that are involved in creating and working in the therapeutic space of symbolic relatedness.

Dr. Albert Rothenberg, an outstanding researcher in the field of creativity, also pays particular attention to the cognitive aspects of creative interventions in treatment (1987). Rothenberg describes two specific modes of creative cognition: "homospatial process," consisting

of actively conceiving two or more discrete entities occupying the same space, and "janusian process," which
is defined as actively conceiving simultaneously two or
more opposite or antithetical entities. Each, he demonstrates, plays a major role in metaphorical and empathic
contact with patients. His material draws heavily on the
disciplines of literature and science, with relatively
minor emphasis placed on the role of the visual and
performing arts. These contributions are enormously
important. A cognitive approach that in effect does not
actively utilize sensuous forms as an organic part of the
treatment process, however, leaves an apparent theoretical vacuum.

Dr. William Confer, in his text *Intuitive Psychotherapy* (1987), also draws heavily on the cognitive creative problem-solving approach to treatment. He
integrates psycholinguistics, information processing,
and social influence theory into this framework.

Similarly, Dr. Gilbert Rose, in his book *Trauma and
Mastery in Life and Art* (1987), weaves a most impressive
thesis of aesthetic form in art and therapy. He offers
examples of creative writers, such as Dostoyevski and
John Fowles, who transformed personal trauma into
mastery through creative expression. He contrasts pathology (as a form of individual artistic expression that
has its own coherence and aesthetics, albeit skewed
and distorted) with the creative work of the artist,
which is far more conscious and integrated. In both
areas of expression, there is an attempt to master personal trauma. Thus, in treatment, the "art form" of the
patient is expressed through transference and enters
the communicative pattern of the ongoing process.
This communicative pattern has its own aesthetic

organization and transformations, which become re-shaped during the treatment process.

Rose, too, acknowledges the importance of the internalization process that transpires between patient and therapist as a facilitator of treatment. He describes the establishment of internalization in the following terms: "(1) through the establishment of a gratifying involvement followed by (2) the experience of incompatibility in that involvement" (Behrends & Blatt, 1985, p. 213). In other words, interactions with others that formerly had been gratifying and then disrupted are transformed into one's own enduring functions and characteristics.

Placing these two theoretical treatment assumptions together and extrapolating, the aesthetics of transitional space becomes a very important factor in aiding the process of identification between patient and therapist, with the identification process itself representing a delicate balance between gratification and frustration. Gratification exists in the form of a deep mirroring resonance, a oneness reminiscent of both the artist's merging with his medium in one phase of creation and also the early relating of mother and child. In therapy, this can be observed by the rhythm, the interplay of inside and outside therapeutic space, the creation of therapeutic empathic metaphors, and the mixing of sensuous forms of nonverbal responses. This nonverbal relatedness is characterized by intonation of voice, postural and facial expressions, and kinesthetic resonance. All these dimensions reflect aspects of primary-process thinking that mirror the force of id drives, or the real "juice" or fuel in a person.

Frustration arises in the form of separateness—the

disruption of the resonance with interpretative interventions to give form and definition to the therapeutic communication. Here, secondary-process thinking is utilized and is similar to the second phase of artistic creation in which the artist distances herself from the artwork to observe and shape the material. When this early resonance is broken, and if the connecting has been "good enough" in a Winnicottian sense, the patient will internalize a connecting transitional symbolic link with the therapist who serves as a stabilizing center for the treatment process. Stated another way, the process of relating and identifying with a significant "other" facilitates the awareness of self.

In essence, therapy can be viewed as an art form that embodies the principles of aesthetics as applied to personal communication and demands the creative use of the therapist's emotional and cognitive resources to promote the patient's own artistry, enabling him to make new forms out of a constant flow of energy and internal symbols that emanate from the treatment process. Shifting back and forth between formlessness and form, unity and separateness, the integration of primary and secondary processes becomes part of the therapeutic creative process. Furthermore, it is the very integration of primary- and secondary-process thinking that gives life to cold, flat communications or organizes communications that spill out disconnectedly from the patient's center.

The core of the patient's self, therefore, consists of formless energy emanating from his center and moving toward form and structure. It is the essence of a personality, often observed at birth and sometimes lost in the various stages of growth. Development within this energetic perspective entails the building of forms that are fed from a center, radiating toward a grid that connects the inner and outer levels of consciousness. (For example, within this framework, death becomes a transitional stage to formlessness.)

In this book, therapeutic issues regarding different levels of consciousness and reality will be elaborated on in Chapter 9, which deals with a patient who struggles with AIDS. Another central theme that unfolds through various chapters places particular emphasis on working with the ego state of blackness. As will be seen, the emotional state of blackness can evolve into any number of forms, ranging from death, sadness, elegance, and power. The ability to find light and luminosity in "blackness" becomes a central thesis associated with therapeutic transcendence. Put simply, the discovery of hope within the heavy black spaces of life becomes an organizing force, fueling a spiritual rebirth of the self.

For these transitions (those regarding art and therapy) to take place, however, the therapist has to be willing to feel the psychic fabric of the therapeutic communicative structure. Like the artist who must know the very texture and character of his material before he or she can create a work of art, so, too, must the therapist feel and touch the very substance of the patient's being, the quality of his or her presence, the very character of his or her armor, before an empathic transitional space can be created or maintained.

The density and use of psychic space and induced images become part of the experience of this fabric, be it soft, crusty, pliable, glasslike and fragile, and so forth. Therefore, it would be simplistic to think of this fabric as a single layer; part of the artistry of therapy involves touching and knowing the various layers and feeling where the patient is at any given time. In addition to knowing the fabric, the therapist must be able to mirror at different levels, both to create an empathic holding environment and to give patients reflections of themselves at different stages during therapy. Sometimes the level of mirroring is more superficial, reflecting the outside, while at other times the mirror goes deeply into the patients' psyches, reflecting nonverbalized and profound pieces of the self. As therapists, we offer a balance or counterbalance to the energy in the relationship, respond sensitively to changing nuances in the transference–countertransference relationship. To do this, we must be able to temporarily lose our boundaries and feel the inner life of our patients— no easy task, given the intense, primitive emotions that may reside there.

Throughout this dance, a variety of images between therapist and patient interplay on both a conscious and unconscious level and create a dynamic interactive art form, or what I call the art therapeutic diptych. When working, the ongoing sessions have an aliveness, integrity, authenticity, and rhythm or balance. Each session becomes a work of art with a theme, the theme weaving in and out of any number of sessions. Just as any artist faces blocks or becomes stale and repetitive, however, so, too, do therapist and patient become lost in the evolving therapeutic process. Stagnation arises from the homeostatic forces within the patient or therapist struggling against the counterforces toward change. The traditional interpretations that normally bring patient and therapist back in sync with one another do not seem to help. While both par-

ties can equally resist the call for change, it is hoped
that the therapist is more in touch with his or her resistance to the unknown, and consciously works to master them. With the so-called difficult patient, i.e., the
borderline, character disorder, schizoid, or paranoid,
powerful introjected forces and projective identifications constantly make their way into the session, often
in subtle, nonverbal communications that can carry violent and intensely painful libidinal and aggressive
forces. For example, with a patient who exhibits masochistic structure, whenever there is movement toward
relatedness, the introject will emerge to break up the
gains, putting the person back in a self-doubting, self-
destructive position. Regardless of the specific nature
of the introject, however, when this uncanny presence
intrudes into the therapeutic relationship, it interferes
with the two parties making empathic contact.

At this juncture, the task of the therapist is to recognize and contain the transmission of the projections
and then to create a means to neutralize and transform
them. This process, often referred to as "working with
the resistance," can shift the therapist's own therapeutic center and therefore requires an emotional "letting
go" of the old therapeutic positions in order to hear and
listen to the patient from a new perspective. During
these transitional periods, a creative leap of sorts is
taken, and old meanings yield a new, better integrated
frame. Again, to use the creative process as an analogy,
when the artist finds him/herself on a plateau, breaking
out of the stalemate requires a shift in figure and
ground, so that old perspectives can be reordered and
reorganized. Occasionally, there is a transcendent shift
in which the jump is not simply to a higher order of

integration, but a giant leap that wipes out old meanings to create a new, more complex reality. This transcendent light of therapy is an infrequent visitor to the therapeutic scene for we usually settle in our efforts, ranging from fair, to average, to occasionally very good. Yet, it is important for us to remember that like being a "good enough" mother, these "good enough" sessions accomplish our treatment goals.

The process of transformation has been described by artist Donna Girasek in conjunction with her print work: Attracted to the image of earth mother, she loses herself in deep, sensuous lines that find their way into a variety of images and symbols; then, as soon as she has completed a drawing or print, she attacks her work with a volley of self-criticism. Out of a deep internal crevice, the "bad mother" has entered the studio and attacks the artist's search for a transformational image. Donna's particular adaptation to a punitive superego is to move from modality to modality so that her internal attacker will not find a stationary target. At one point, Donna shows me a print (Figure 3) that she considers a failure. As I peruse the work, I share with her my observation that it looks wicked and evil and that I am impressed with its power. At first, she is unable to perceive the symbol; but slowly the image emerges for her, and the material takes on a new reality. Perhaps her constant search for the earth mother has interfered with a deeper merging of primary-process material. As we talk, we draw parallels to therapy, where both patient and therapist are locked in a transference–countertransference relationship of good mother (therapist)/ hungry child (patient) rather than therapist and patient mutually exploring their respective evilness.

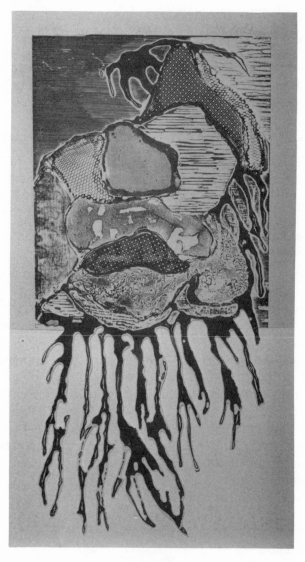

FIGURE 3

After our interview, Donna returns home and feels as if she has been released from a psychic prison. From this point, she takes giant steps in exploring the evil part of herself in her artwork as well as in her relationship with her husband. Suddenly the feeling tone of power emerges out of this integration (Figures 3, 4, and 5).

Christopher Bollas (1987) speaks of the transformational object in the following terms:

> ...I have termed the early mother a "transformational object" and the adult's search for transformation constitutes in some respects a memory of this early relationship. There are other memories of this period of life, such as aesthetic experience, when a person feels uncannily embraced by an object.

In this brief example, using Donna Girasek's artwork, we can see how plumbing the deeper symbolic depths of one's existence leads to not only an aesthetic wholeness, but also to a rediscovery of the "transformational object."

Bollas describes the "aesthetic moment" as that moment when the individual experiences a deep subjective rapport with an object, and feels an uncanny fusion with the object. This fusion is not necessarily always benign, for in treatment, the aesthetic moment may occur at the depths of mutual despair, when both therapist and patient hit the emotional boundary of treatment. When both participants share their mutual distress, the opportunity arises for therapeutic reordering of space. In this joining, though sometimes painful, the boundaries become more pliable and hope emerges.

The ability to oscillate from an ego state of form to

FIGURE 4

FIGURE 5

formlessness substantially contributes to the therapist's capacity to contain, organize, and process projective identifications. A tightly controlled therapeutic stance, as manifested by a controlled, detached demeanor in the therapist, will invariably interfere with his or her ability to feel the essence of subtle latent forces at play. On the other hand, the therapist's loose boundaries can substantially contribute to muddiness and lack of conceptual clarity. Ideally, a state of "free-floating attention" should be maintained, a state not easy to hang on to when assaulted daily by the potentially overwhelming introjects of patients. Needless to say, the better acquainted the therapist is with his or her own "demons," the easier it will be to work with the powerful introjects of others. Despite the therapist's state of preparedness, however, the constant battling with introjects and the ongoing painful identifications that must be found within himself/herself in order to make deep emotional connections with patients take their toll, periodically knocking the best of therapists off center. If therapists are to remain effective and not prematurely burn out, support groups, where it is possible to vent rage and upsets and regain equilibrium, become necessary.

There are no easy methods or answers to help us facilitate the conversion of evil introjects or defenses into strengths for our patients. Each therapist must develop his or her own unique aesthetic style in processing and responding to this subcurrent of forces. What works in one situation does not work in another seemingly similar therapeutic dialogue. Therapeutic artistry takes precedence over scientific acumen. Such intangible factors as the therapist's use of tone, reflection,

rhythm, and cognitive style will make or break movement at such difficult junctures. As is true of the artist
who must combine aesthetic discipline with his or her
personal style, so too must the therapist find a style
that merges his or her personality (complete with characteristic defenses) with the discipline of sound therapeutic technique and aesthetic principles. At the point
in therapy when an interpretation is presented, it must
be connected to the affective undercurrents in the treatment relationship. A good interpretation addresses
both verbal content and nonverbal messages and is
couched in terms appropriate to developmental
considerations.

The therapist, then, must create a bridge to transform a resistance or barrier into a path leading somewhere new. The concept of bridges involves moving
from signs to symbols. All too often, patients hide behind linear dialogues. Once they experience symbolic
relatedness, they move into a transitional space—that
"place" where many levels of meaning come together.
An exercise with art therapy students demonstrates
this point. The students were asked to draw a bridge.
Though not explicitly stated, I was interested in exploring the visual metaphor that is analogous to the verbal
functions of interpretation through the symbol of the
bridge. One student reported that her bridge was
sunny, with trees, but that she was basically left cold
and unmoved by it and by the exercise. I then asked her
to think of a "crazy" bridge. She immediately presented
the image of a wooden bridge with a rope railing going
from one cliff to another. She was still rather unmoved
by this image, but when I asked her where this bridge
was located and she identified it as being in Jamaica,

her birthplace, her eyes became teary and her immobile face broke into a smile. An emotional connection was made. The image connected to a deeper source of energy, and a piece of her emotional center became connected with the sadness and joy in her current reality. Another student created a prosaic bridge that was full of pastoral nuances. In describing her picture, she expressed the feeling of lassitude, and looked forward to a vacation at the end of the term. Once again I requested that she think of a crazy bridge. Her mind turned to the Brooklyn Bridge, crowded with bums and covered by pollution. Could this polluted, dirty part enter her prosaic, naturalistic drawing, I asked. She agreed to try, and suddenly her prosaic bridge became alive with dimensionality.

For some students, the crazy bridge had no beginning and no end, as they were in a period of transition, going from being students to professionals. All of these bridges made a poignant connection.

To another class I offered a somewhat different set of instructions. This time I requested a crazy bridge for the initial exercise. The students reported that it was fun, as groups of three students worked to create triptychs. The artwork was lively and quite original, and very different from the first set of drawings from the other class. Students in the second class were certain that if I had not presented the instructions as I had done, the resultant drawings would have been different. We observe here how styles of playing with image and form can reflect a variety of ego rhythms in artistic expression.

Patient communications, for the most part, are neither elegant nor artistic when expressing symbolic form. I recall an art therapy student who complained one day in class, "What do you do with acting-out kids who make one hamburger after another out of clay?" I asked what this hamburger needed to gain aesthetic appeal. The student mockingly replied, "A bun...fat chance. Ask him to put a bun on it and he'll destroy the clay even more." "Ah," I responded, "but at least your awareness that the hamburger needs a bun is the aesthetic impetus to translate problems from an aesthetic perspective to psychodynamic language. What would happen if you reflected to the child that the hamburger seemed lonely for a bun?" "His reply would be to pound the hamburger even further into smithereens," she said. "And what better way," I said, "to elicit his rage." This pounding harbors the beginning of a new ego rhythm that seeks expression and understanding through angry drumbeats.

What we are often doing in building bridges is playing with the tension between primary and secondary processes, and helping our patients to do the same. What we often see is either too much primary process, and with it a flooding of affect, or too much secondary process, and with it too much control. Finding a balance gives meaning with feeling and releases a creative, generative power. Our job as therapists is to create a climate (draw a "crazy bridge") that encourages the amplification of a sign into a symbol. The inner symbolic connections of the therapist who provides the image threads that build sensory traces into full, rich, cognitive experiences are thus involved.

These emotional bridges between therapist and patient, commonly called transitional space, promote the possibilities of a holding environment that can both contain and metabolize toxic affects. The merging of the therapeutic and creative processes becomes the challenge for both parties. First, however, the therapist must experience the pain of the identification with the patient's internal conflicts as well as the anguish of the separation that is inherent in the therapist's personal processing of associations and affects. Through this linking, a gradual calm and centeredness often develops within the therapist as there becomes a greater sense of personal space for both therapist and patient. In the meantime, the toxic affects have found a more connective cognitive thread in terms of the patient's past and present. The therapist offers a new perspective to the material at hand, which most importantly offers the possibilities of self-acceptance. At times, the patient's character armor can be rediscovered as offering new strength and adaptiveness. Hopefully, out of this matrix, toxicity becomes transformed into a benign acceptance of one's pain and existence. In short, there is a therapeutic trade-off: The therapist contains the patient's self-hate while offering in turn self-love through an empathic relatedness.

As has been described in the above paragraphs, treatment on its most profound level is a constant emotional challenge for both patient and therapist, and at times calls forth in the therapist the need to be an active participant in his or her own personal therapy.

Now let's place some of these notions within a clinical perspective. The first case I will describe has created for me more than its share of personal struggles.

Linda had been in treatment for over three years on a four-times-weekly basis. At times I wondered what we were both doing in treatment, and whether she should have been transferred to another therapist long ago. I suspect that my sense of embarrassment and discomfort with this case says something about the dynamics and inductions that are so much a part of Linda's life story.

Linda came from an extremely deprived background. I have quietly wondered with awe how a person can survive circumstances like Linda's where there has been so little love and care. Linda's family included a [set of twin] sister[s] who was [were] 16 months younger than she. Linda reported with bitterness and anguish how her younger sister was consistently treated as the favorite child. At first I was suspicious and wary of her statements, for I found it hard to believe that there could be such a complete split with the patient painted all black and the sister all white. Yet everything she told me had a ring of truth. Her mother seemed to have created a classic split in the family, viewing the sister as more sociable, friendly, and lovable. From Linda's description, the mother had always remarked that from the outset Linda was cranky, sour, and depressed. Linda, then, became the recipient of the mother's split-off scorn and self-hatred. One memory remains etched in my mind: Linda would sit on the kitchen table as a small child, begging her mother to answer her plea, "Do you love me? Do you love me?" The mother, in turn, would laugh until Linda was reduced to tears. The mother, seemingly an extremely narcissistic, self-involved, insensitive person, was happy to stay away from the children, and made it her business to be out working when they were home from school. This was often dangerous, as the children were left without babysitters. Aside from being self-involved, the mother spent a considerable amount of time keeping things neat and clean rather than attending to the emotional needs of her family. It was not hard to believe then, as Linda reported, that she had been completely toilet trained by the age of 9 months. Though this seems almost impossible, I had no reason to doubt its veracity. Very early in her life, Linda became subject to massive hives. At the age of 8, she was sent to California to live with an aunt when the mother was hospitalized due to a schizophrenic breakdown. And so, for a brief period, Linda lived in a supportive, comfortable environment. She rarely heard from her mother and father during this time, but, in spite of the strange new environment, things felt much better in this new life. After a year, she returned home to the conditions she had left behind; the small respite (the year spent in California) would become an important anchor to which she would often refer for the rest of her life.

Her father was apparently equally unloving, being described as tight, controlled, and angry. Linda said it was like living at the edge of a volcano. At first she had some positive feelings toward this man. At least, she remembers having run to the door to greet him when he came home from work. Somewhere around the age of 10 or 11, this all changed. Linda remembered her father hugging her until she physically hurt and cried. She decided at that point to avoid him as much as possible, and can't remember feeling any remorse or regret when he died. Linda's adolescence was spent in her room reading books, cloistered and protected from her family; her sister, on the other hand, had made many friends and was part of a teenage group. Linda's father had resisted her desire to attend college; he felt that she should get married and raise a family. Somehow, in spite of his resistance, Linda prevailed. Between a scholarship from the college and her own hard work, she was able to extricate herself from her home to attend classes.

During her young adult years, Linda, though wary of men, was pleased by their attention. She was a fairly good-looking woman and attracted a number of young men, but the whole field of sexual engagement was frightening. Fortune seemed to have smiled on her when it came to marriage. She gravitated toward a man who basically was warm and supportive. At first, she questioned the intensity of her feelings, but at the same time knew that he loved her, which made her feel secure and protected in the relationship.

Over the years, through much testing, Linda started to trust her husband and developed a deep caring and love for him. After marriage Linda attended law school, working during the day and attending classes at night. She acquired a private practice after working for a number of law firms. Her work remained fairly marginal. Along the way, she raised her children, two boys, who in spite of some problems seemed to be able to find their own way as they grew up. In spite of all this, Linda approached treatment feeling like a professional failure. She came into treatment with work issues as her focus.

The basic problems of transference and countertransference were stormy, to say the least. Linda interjected into our treatment relationship a sense of disconnection and aloneness that required recognition and attention. Every vacation period I took from treat-

ment was a stormy one. At first, the rage regarding her
sense of desertion was deflected onto her husband, but
it soon entered into our treatment relationship. Eventually, I would develop rage and an enormous fury toward her. I wasn't quite sure how it happened, but
invariably, nearing a vacation period, there was an enormous amount of tension and pressure in the room. She
became closed off, provocative, belittling, angry, and
demanding, and I in turn felt impotent, furious, and
disconnected. At times we worked out of this bind by a
direct interpretive approach. I would describe her
sense of desertion, her fury, the projections of her own
impotence and rage into our relationship as having
come from that rage and impotence she had felt
throughout her life. During these periods she was often
on the verge of walking out or withholding payment,
feeling cheated, angry, and yet attached and unable to
do anything about her relationship with me. She saw
treatment as a masochistic surrender of whatever sense
of self she had, feeling she was hooked on a drug, being unable to assert herself, and hating herself and me
for her dependency. She wanted to feel special, and yet
felt like everyone else, just one more patient.

Many of these issues improved over the course of
treatment, and she became far less depressed and more
related and connected to herself. Yet the ruthless volley
of self-attacks on her worth still invaded the room as
she attempted to work through both her wish for and
fear of intimacy. At each step, as she moved closer to
me, there was the echo of her mother intruding on our
relationship, cutting off relatedness and creating a volley of self-deprecating attacks. Each one of these inci-
dents, I believed, had been used transferentially as a

way of testing whether I could handle and accept her self-hatred, her sense of being unlovable, and her need to be appreciated. As I write this material, I can still hear the volley of self-assaults: "I am dumb, I am stupid, I should get out of my profession," or, "People are laughing at me and mock me behind my back."

For the most part, I attempted to interpret this material in terms of the mother's presence constantly interfering with her wish for intimacy and warmth with me, yet her self-attacks continued relentlessly. From time to time there developed a working alliance between us as she attempted to control her self-attacks. She became aware of the fused connection between her mother and herself, with her acting out of her mother's self-hatred. Yet, at crucial periods in her life, particularly as she made progress, the self-attacks returned.

At a very crucial point in treatment my tolerance and patience for these self-attacks had reached more than their limit. I found myself becoming increasingly furious at being the unwitting partner to these masochistic assaults. I stood by helplessly watching her tear herself apart, my interpretations ineffective in stopping this behavior. Finally, in spite of myself, I burst out after one of these barrages of self-attack, complaining: "Enough, enough, no more self-attacks. They are not helpful or therapeutic. Enough is enough." She quickly replied, "What do you expect? You can't stand me, you hate me. You want to get rid of me. I've always known that even though you've tried to be therapeutic. You really can't stand my guts and are happy to get rid of me. What is more, you are like all men: self-centered and only interested in yourself. Aren't you supposed to understand my feelings?" She then bitterly continued:

"This is who I am. What are you telling me—that I cannot talk about myself and how I feel? This is how I really feel. I feel like getting up and walking out, and only because it would give you extra time, I won't give you that satisfaction. I don't want to give you anything."

I am really not sure where my response came from, for I was not consciously thinking about what to say and nothing came to my mind. The words rolled from a deep place inside myself. I told her that I was observing a small child being brutalized, and continued: "You are asking me to sit by helplessly while this child is beaten up. I cannot watch this being done to you any more. For you to keep doing this to yourself is tantamount to my participating in this assault." While offering these connections, I became aware of vague affects and flashes coming into my consciousness. Memories of a thin, slumped-over boy, all too frightened and inadequate, became a party to my patient's pain. Slowly, the memories and affects gave way to a sense of personal separateness from the patient. She was quiet and thoughtful for a while, and spoke in soft tones about her lack of protection throughout her life. I now felt the beginning of an important shift in our relationship. Perhaps it was an aesthetic moment, for both of us moved into a healing space. Yet, this very strong self-destructive force did not suddenly go away, since in future sessions the assaults on herself returned. But something very dramatic did happen: The area of sexual intimacy in the transference, an area she had avoided for many sessions, now emerged. She spoke about her sexual love, and how it felt, and the feelings she held for me were deep, tender, and erotic. I won-

dered if she was talking to the protective father who
would rescue her from her mother. Linda continued to
talk about her feelings and at first I made no interpretation as to what was going on. She was wary of her sexual feelings and of talking about them. She complained
that they all seemed rather pornographic, and she felt
vulnerable. She noted, "You don't feel the same." She
continued and complained, "I know you have the right
answers, that you are here to understand me, but I
want something more; I want to be special. I want to
have sex with you because I want to drink in your
power through my vagina." She persisted with these
strong feelings, and in the process complained of feeling humiliated and dissected in the analytic process. I
commented that sexuality for her was a very humiliat-
ing experience, since she was taking a considerable risk
in opening up to the transference father who she experienced on a very brittle, violent level. I decided to take
a strong stand and continued to confront this repetitive
deadness that encased our relationship, characterized
by these sadomasochistic assaults on herself. Linda had
lived all too long in darkness, and required light—an
authentic responsiveness on my part—in order to deal
with the stale repetitiousness of her self-inflicted pain.
Perhaps there had been an acting out on my part af-
fording some degree of transference gratification in my
being the protective father; yet, I also believe that somewhere a part of both of us met on an extremely important level, and that a sense of specialness was partially
realized when I said to her, "Enough, I will not stand
by helplessly and observe your self-inflicted pain."

In this brief interchange, I have described the
transformational process in treatment—the mirroring

of the anguish and pain that was destroying the very fabric of one individual's existence. Linda's "mother" was being confronted and the therapeutic mirror was no longer an interpretive reflection. The anguish and pain of the child was being experienced by both Linda, the patient, and myself, the therapist. The wish for a protective father who would save her from the mother was also *felt*. The patient was now joined by an ally who could stand up to the introjected mother.

Here, as equal participants, struggling with our mutual distress, we attempted to hear one another. Paradoxically, I *was* being authoritarian when I voiced, "I have had enough of this stale repetitiousness." I had reached my limit as to what I felt I could possibly bear, but I do not believe that my analytic role was compromised; rather, I was making a therapeutic statement that would prove helpful in preserving our therapeutic alliance. I was affirming, in effect, "you have a right to exist without assault. You have a right to live, and I am here to protect that."

I thought about this session for quite a while, particularly about my role as a therapist. As I continue to reflect, it occurs to me that much of the work done with therapy patients is neither transcendent nor transformational in nature. We work with defenses, analyze resistance, and provide a frame around which patients can put together a story of their life. Yet, there is much that goes on between patient and therapist that is beyond interpretation: we soothe, we affirm, we validate, but also we heal. Every so often, though, as with the session just reported, something very special happens: the therapist and patient make a core-level connection where there is an experience of the meeting of the minds. Some might interpret it as a level of selflessness, of being so present and vulnerable that the character armor of both parties has been stripped away. In this state of healing, where two minds meet on this very deep level, the potential for transformation arises.

Linda's very fabric of psychic existence was pained as well as vulnerable and full of rage. My communications were of equal tenor, mixed with softness and soothing, always keeping a clear sense of my therapeutic boundaries.

In contrast to the above case, I now offer another clinical example. Here, the communication matrix is of a different order and cadence, and the reader can see how the therapeutic beat is mirrored as each transition phase unfolds.

Joe had been in treatment with three other therapists before he came to see me. All had helped, but still he struggled with core issues of self-doubt and despair. Joe presented a paradox; he was, on the one hand, lively, funny, and engaging, but on the other hand, he would often suffer deep states of despair and emptiness. At times he seemed virtually unreachable in treatment, having nothing he thought worth saying, and wanting just to be with me in silence. He reported that at home he often sat in an empty unfurnished apartment and lost himself watching his television set. On other occasions he'd lose himself in work. He was a lawyer who spent long hours working for his firm, resenting the time and the pressure, always wanting very much to be approved of by his superiors, sometimes wanting to leave, and other times wanting to be promoted to a position of partner. The latter he sometimes felt would be the ticket to being recognized and affirmed, although he also doubted that was possible. Joe, though feeling deeply inadequate and unworthy of love, wore the business suits required by his position and had bought an apartment in the city. But, in spite of these efforts, the apartment reflected a deep and telling statement about his life. He lived in empty rooms with a mattress on the floor. While in therapy with me, Joe finally decided to employ an interior decorator to help him put some richness and comfort into his living quarters.

Joe's life, we observe, is a metaphor of his existence. He is funny, but also pained and in anguish.

In brief, Joe's background includes a father who basically performed a great deal of mothering, but who was viewed as narcissistic and self-serving. He wanted nothing but the best for the son, as long as the "best" was in terms of the father's own aspirations. The mother seemed out of the picture; she may have been overwhelmed with running the house and satisfying Joe's father and an older brother. The father apparently played the dominant role. In his youth, Joe attempted to live up to his father's expectations, but in early adulthood could not sustain this and lapsed into long periods of despair. Many years were spent trying to extricate himself from the father's influence, but he was unable to do this completely. He feared rejection by women and doubted his ability to satisfy them. He was dissatisfied with work since it absorbed his very existence, and though he fought it, found himself usually succumbing to its demands.

His sense of humor helped him go on. When people responded to his humor positively he would become alive and present. But despite the humor, which was often provocative, alive, and engaging, he was often very sad and raw.

Humor, then, was an important part of treatment. Through the humor we touched and yet still preserved distance with one another. Sometimes, as in the session described below, the humor led to a more direct, creative exploration of his deepest wishes and fears. In the following description of one of our sessions, you can see our interchange as we bantered yet maintained an aura of deadly seriousness.

I remind Joe that this session will be taped. I had not taped any sessions in some time. Joe asked, "How come the tape is on this time and not other times?" I replied, rather nonchalantly, that I would be swamped with tapes if I attempted to tape every session. Joe immediately replied: "Maybe you shouldn't tape this. Who knows what I'll say?" He then cajoled me, "How are you going to publish this in a serious scientific journal? There doesn't seem to be a consistent methodology, taping some sessions and not others. Don't you have an experimental plan?" "No," I replied, in the same vein, "I'll improvise as I go along." "How," he asked provocatively, "is a respectable journal going to take this?" "Well maybe," I said, "this will have to go in a not-so-respectable journal." "I know," he said, "I know. But I don't want my tapes to be in some schlock journal," and we both laughed. "Well," Joe said, "maybe we can find a journal called the *Journal for Schlock Psychology.*" And I retorted, "Well, there has to be a place for schlock psychology, too."

He then wanted to know if this was going to be an article or part of a book, and when I said that I didn't quite know as yet, he asked, "So what's the idea behind this?" I commented, in brief, that I was going to go over sessions and try to understand what went on between therapist and patient. He replied, again with a kind of laughing, mocking voice, "This should be on video. How are you going to capture all the nuances?" I agreed, but continued, saying that the tape would give me enough to recall what had gone on in the session. "Well, like what?" he said. "Well, as we talk now I'll remember the look on your face. It looks mischievous, provocative, peaceful, a little wary and suspicious." "How are you going to remember all that on a tape?" "I'll just have to do the best I can."

I knew we were talking, through metaphor, about whether I would really listen and see and care about his communication and life, but I was not ready to intrude and stop the banter. He needed this vehicle to continue. Joe went on: "Should I stop every 5 minutes and give you a chance to copy down some comments about the nonverbal work?" He laughed. "I'll just try to remember," I said, "as best I can. I have a pretty good memory." "How are you going to put down such things as (he's putting his finger in his mouth) or things like that? Are you going to describe how you have your feet on the desk and your hands right behind your head?" Then he quipped to the tape machine, "You got that?"

"I should have a desk, too, where I could put my feet up, and just act like you are—the boss. And you are always telling me that this is my session. It's my session as long as I pay, then I can do whatever I want." I interjected, "I said that? I wasn't sure I said you could do whatever you want. I said that you could say whatever you want." "Well," Joe replied in the same bantering tone, "isn't this symbolic speech?" "So," I said,

"I'm expressing my bossiness." He replied, "Well, I should have something where I can put my feet up too." And he added, "And you probably won't let me put my feet up as high as yours. And you said that you're not interested in power." I replied in a whimsical way, "I said that? I didn't say that. If I did, I was a liar." "How can I trust you, when you lie on top of it?" "Well," I said, "You'll just have to accept my foibles. Certainly I'm interested in power, who isn't?" "All you need," he said, "is a cigar." "Well," I said, "that wouldn't be half bad, and maybe some day you'll have your cigar." "And then," he joined in, "I'd be complete." "So here I am," I said, "with my feet up on the desk and my cigar in my mouth, speaking to one of my employees." He replied, "No, I am not an employee, I am one of your associates." "One day," I said, "you'll become partner." Joe retorted, "And I'll have a cigar, too." We were giggling and laughing about this, but there was a good deal of seriousness behind what we were saying to each other.

"What shall we entitle this session?" Joe asked. "Perhaps," I said, "we will dedicate this session to those patients who serve, and you can put this in the *Journal of Schlock Psychology. Schlock Psychology Today*, by Arthur Robbins and his servile patients." There was a long sigh, and I wondered if I had played too hard with the dialogue. Then Joe said more seriously, "You know you ought to take your feet off the table." I readily agreed and proceeded to do so. He then said, "You know, this is my fourth year coming here, and I'm not sure what we've just accomplished." I recognized that he was wondering if all this banter helped, and what we actually accomplished through this, but I decided to see where he would go with the material, and maintained the pitter patter.

I said, "Well, you have a nice apartment." He said, "Yes, but it's empty." "You have a TV set," I said. "Well, that's questionable. I have a job," he continued, "but now I have to maintain this apartment." I interjected, "Where are we going to go from here?" He then said seriously, "What I'd like to do is to get a job I don't find so overpowering, and a girl, someone who I can care for."

The mood now had shifted palpably. The very fast interplay and banter ceased and Joe became more serious, to share something important. He started to talk to me about a comedian on WBAI, Mike Feder, who told personal, often psychological, and sometimes inspiring stories. "It's kind of like a sermon," he said. "He talks about all kinds of things and he is the kind of man who has a background similar to mine—crazy mother coming from Queens. By talking about Santa Claus, and whether there really is a Santa Claus, he opens up a very deep issue, something like Judy Garland singing 'Over the Rainbow.' I'm not sure that there is such a rainbow, but it's something that touches me inside. He's talking in this kind of way as he puts records on; he talks sincerely in a kind of crazy way. It's something that made quite an impression, and makes me feel good."

Joe went on for the rest of the session, talking about some things that had happened in his life. He spoke about asking out a secretary in his office, and although she didn't want to date him, it was important that he was able to do what he wanted to do and at least ask her out. He spoke about his working hard over the weekend; of sometimes getting lost in watching television; and of other women to whom he attempted to make overtures. He spoke about the sadness that he could no longer be the good boy, for there was no longer anyone in his life who would make everything okay— only the mortal man behind the machine, who was indeed no Wizard of Oz. In these brief aesthetic moments, he was alive and engaged with the inner self. During the last half hour the tone of the session had changed: The jokes and the fun had subsided. The pain of recognition had entered into his awareness.

The metaphor, "somewhere over the rainbow" became the theme of this session. Indeed, there was no Wizard of Oz, no powerful parent who would protect him and take him back to his roots. All that remained was a mortal masquerading as the Wizard. This seemed to describe the nature of our relationship. I was merely his "schlock psychologist"; and yet there was a life to deal with in spite of the disillusionment. Feeling the fabric of this patient, recognizing it, enjoying it, and participating in it, became a blanket within which Joe felt accepted enough so that he could dare to express his sense of inner vulnerability and despair. A more direct, linear interpretation would only serve as a painful reminder of his deep wound and injury.

The term "fabric of the patient" seems appropriate language for such therapeutic issues as the self. In this particular clinical example, the external fabric of Joe's professional life seemed strongly webbed and tight, but the internal fabric was more fragile and delicate, but perhaps also more beautiful. I avoided applying too much pressure to this material, for such pressure probably would have led to the fabric knotting into silence, or perhaps even falling apart. Feeling this fabric, moving into it and understanding its weave, became an open invitation for the patient to see its beauty and reorganize and sew the quilt of his existence into his own new pattern. As Joe's fabric became tighter and more finely knit, we could look more closely at the gaping holes in his past.

In the ensuing chapters, I will discuss in depth the process of empathic relatedness that is analogous to a highly artistic style of communication. In this process, there are both verbal and nonverbal forms that have filtered through a permeability of the analyst's boundaries and can be described as a dual level of consciousness. Here, the therapist is both one with his patient and separate. The therapist constantly organizes sensory and symbolic material into both cognitive and sensuous forms and transmits these through therapeutic expressions of metaphors, a variety of nonverbal resonances, and rather straightforward, organized, verbal interpretations. The patient likewise responds to this material on both verbal and nonverbal levels. Thus, through the real relationship, the therapist facilitates a cohesive organization of transitional space that is constantly being challenged by the artwork, or transference communications, of the patient. The organization of aesthetic form that goes on in the real relationship, therefore, parallels, complements, mirrors, or opposes the patient's work of art. We have therefore two art forms simultaneously interacting in treatment and also a number of transformational processes in which these two art forms become one, eventually merging into a larger and more dynamic picture of life. This larger picture is not created easily, for both parties must transcend the reality of the transference to maintain a new mastery and aesthetic organization of pain. Put another way, if the art form of the patient originally develops out of an attempt to transform pain, then it is left to the analyst to combine sound "scientific" knowledge of theory and technique in addition to his own artistry in order to meet the challenge of facilitating new pathways for the patient to transform pain into mastery.

In this therapeutic amalgamation of art and science we observe a deterioration of aesthetic form as the antiartistic nature of the patient disorganizes the constructive–communicative elements of treatment. The antiartist, however, does not reside solely in the intrapsychic fabric of the patient. As therapists, we, too, are human and therefore vulnerable to the dissociative pressures of a socioeconomic spatial matrix. Our patients as well as our practice must invariably mirror the antiartist that can destroy any communication that emanates from the "therapeutic center" and automatically takes away from the professional aesthetic self.

This issue will be elaborated on in the final chapter of this book. It is important to note here that a purely scientific approach to psychotherapy mirrors a broader societal issue of fear and suspicion of psychological artistry. Paradoxically, it therefore becomes an artistic challenge for the practitioner to navigate within the borders of social, economic, and scientific pressures and at the same time to preserve the authentic professional self that is so necessary to accomplish the therapeutic task.

At once beguiling and challenging, the union of these two giants, art and science, must combine the humanity of the analyst with the powerful tools of knowledge, organization, and structure. This text aims, then, to offer clues as to the melding of the aesthetics of treatment into the scientific discipline of psychoanalysis so that, as such, it can gain some authenticity.

Each artist views the ebb and flow of energy through their particular medium. The working with and attention to this oscillation becomes a living, breathing experience of being in the art form. Chapter 3, "Ego Rhythm in Art and Therapy," will amplify this process.

2

The Language of the Artist Applied to the Psychotherapeutic Matrix

Introduction

In the next three sections, a dancer, a musician, and a dramatist, each trained as a depth-oriented therapist, will offer their particular metaphor applied to the aesthetics of a verbal psychotherapeutic dialogue. Each emphasizes a particular aspect of the psychotherapeutic matrix. All of them, however, have in common a belief in the psychoaesthetic importance of the therapist–patient interchange.

In the preface of my book, *Expressive Therapy: A Creative Arts Approach to Depth-Oriented Treatment* (1981), I stated the following:

> In any one session, we can detect in patient–therapist communications both verbal and nonverbal cues that

can be examined within the artistic parameters of sight, sound, and motion; that is, in rhythm, pitch, and timbre, in color, texture, and form, and in muscular tension, energy, and special relations. These elements of therapeutic composition have their own principles and require the utmost skill in therapeutic management.

This nonverbal composition of a given patient's communication takes place on a number of psychic levels and presents a unique aesthetic character. First, however, let me define what I mean by aesthetic. In *The Artist as Therapist* (Robbins, 1987), I stated the following:

> When I speak of aesthetics, I'm referring to making the inanimate animate, giving form to diffuse energy or ideas, breathing life into sterile communications. *Communication* is a key word here, for a complete work of any medium becomes art only when it touches us as a living truth. This happens when it is an authentic expression of the artist, and more often it involves an integration of polarities.

In another section, I further elaborate on this point:

> When symbolic form includes multiple levels of communication and transcends its individual parts to communicate a larger meaning, it approaches the level of aesthetic communication.

Historically, the language of the artist has always addressed itself to the self that cannot easily be reduced to words. In the following sections, each artist will offer his/her special view of the language of art applied to the therapist's grappling with an understanding of man's wish to give freedom and space to the very essence of where the self lives.

Movement Composition and the Choreography of a Verbal Psychotherapy Session
Eileen Serlin

P moved against the far wall. She stayed in the corner, keeping 4 or 5 feet between herself and the other group members, not acknowledging them in her movements. She was hunched up, eyes closed, energy pulling inward, hands gesticulating. These hands seemed to flail out into empty space, hands curled like claws, clawing the air. Her head was tilted toward one side, eyes beseeching and flaring, mouth twitching.

She says she wants to be touched, but is terrified and furious. She grew up in an orphanage and was sexually abused as a child. She is afraid of being violated and abandoned.

P's back was to the wall, braced by the wall. This was the only solid point of contact, of support. Everything else was flailing, desperately, helplessly, uselessly. Her body was limp and lacked a strong central inner support.

I momentarily saw my cat, a frightened creature. My cat loves to be held, but if approached tentatively, head-on, with hesitancy, she'll lash out and claw. If approached from the side, however, with swift sureness, decisiveness, and a firm touch, she will melt and cuddle.

I swiftly approached P. Without pause, I moved in from the side and placed my two palms against her thrashing hands. She pushed my hands away. As she pushed, her body resisted, strengthened, and focused. Her flaccid weight mobilized, her diffuse efforts organized. She pushed, and I pushed back. As we pressed

against each other her inward-pulling energy reversed
and flowed toward me. As I stayed steady and clear,
she continued to mobilize her efforts toward me, integrating and mobilizing herself.

Suddenly she screamed—uncanny screams, one
after another. Then she fell sideways, across my lap. I
leaned over her, pressing my upper body down on her,
containing her with my body. Her thrashing diminished, her body quieted, and her tears stopped. She
looked at me and said softly: "Thank you."

What happened during this session? P is a borderline personality, with issues of early maternal deprivation, trust, splitting, and boundaries. Although I
worked with her nonverbally, I believe that elements
which I used to sense our interaction are ones which
can be used to understand a verbal session. These elements—body, space, time, and energy—are from the
language of dance and describe basic compositional
elements of any diagnostic or interactional process.

The language used in most traditional psychology
comes from a mechanistic, Cartesian system that posits
discrete entities, such as ego and id, or which suggests
that dance is about a body literally projecting itself
through space. Modern physics, however, has shown
the world to be more fluid than this. From a non-Carte-
sian perspective, a study of the human mind would
describe processes rather than entities and qualities
rather than quantities. These processes and qualities
are already in movement; movement is basic to life.
Using the language and images of dance can thus help
to articulate patterns of any process. What are the elements of a dance language and how can they be used to

describe the therapeutic process? I will first describe the elements as concretely manifest in the session with P, then I will show how these elements can be used metaphorically to understand the compositional aspects of a therapeutic process.

Body

1. Body parts. Body parts means which parts of the body are emphasized in the movement and how they are used. P used primarily her hands, head, mouth, and eyes. Her hands were like claws, curled inward, arms crooked, head at an angle, mouth grimacing as though she were vomiting, and eyes fixed and glaring. Her torso was concave and still. The shapes of the body parts were in complex angles, convoluted and twisted.

2. Organization. Organization describes how the parts are organized into one moving piece. P's body seemed all joints. The parts did not move together as one organized system, but moved in fragments. A clear, organizing center was missing.

3. Posture. Posture describes the organization of the large architectural units of the body. P's back was supported by the wall. She was not able to maintain an upright posture without this support. With the support, however, she could sustain a great deal of peripheral activity.

4. Flow. Flow is the movement of energy through the body parts and joints. Movement flowed through P's body in a twisting, grinding, circling, spiraling motion, successively moving through the joints.

Space

1. Perspective. If these movements took place in a composition, how would the composition be arranged? P chose to position herself in a far corner of the room, squeezed into the line between floor and wall. She was far from the others in the group and from me. She looked as though she were being seen through a telescope, appearing far away and huddled small.

2. Open versus closed. What is the basic spatial configuration along the dimension of open or closed? P's body was twisted into itself and did not open out to others. Her flailing hands created a wall of "static," a shield of chaos through which penetration to her heart or body center would be difficult.

3. Kinaesphere. How large is the "personal space" bubble in which the mover moves? P claimed a large area as her own space, and her movements did not echo anyone else's or invite anyone into her space. This personal space was clearly hers and not shared.

4. Boundaries. Boundaries refer to the outline or edges of the movement. P's hands kept circling. They did not seem to come up against anything or suggest any edges. There was a sense of her inner self pouring out without a firm container to hold the writhing torment.

5. Negative space. What is the relation of mass to surrounding (negative) space? If P's body were seen as a sculpture, the space around her would be an empty void. There was not a dynamic interplay of matter and space, an interpenetration of shapes. The space around P did not support or contain her; she seemed lost in space, diffuse, alone.

6. Relationship to objects in space. Do P's move-

ments reach out toward others, make clear or vague paths through space? P did not carve through space or reach with intentionality or purpose toward any other individuals. Her efforts to cope with her environment and with others were minimal.

7. Pathways of contact. If contact were to be made, what logical approach would the movement suggest? P's frontal movement blocks and her glaring eyes said not to approach head-on. When, in fact, one of the group members asked if she could approach, P refused, and the group member said that she would have approached too directly. A clear, indirect, peripheral path to P would reach her without threatening her and would establish strong contact at her boundary.

Energy

Energy describes the qualitative (light–strong, quick–slow, direct–indirect, bound–free) and directional aspects of the movement. P's efforts were predominantly light, sustained, very bound, and indirect. The flow of energy pulled inward, referring back to the body center. The loops of movement were repetitive and of even intensity, lacking clear phrasing or closure.

Interaction

What was my own sense of body, space, and energy and how did I use my force field to create a therapeutic dance with P?

First, I sensed her as very far away, as if I were looking at her through a telescope. She felt remote and unreachable. I inched closer, just trying to feel her proximity. As I noticed her against the wall, I felt a need for her to be supported. I had the sense that if I could slither around quickly enough, I could brace her back with my own. But I knew that I could not get there and establish very firm contact fast enough to forestall a reaction. Therefore, I planted myself instead in my own spot and grounded myself by strengthening my own spine and its relation to the floor. From this stable sitting position, I could observe her increasingly agitated movement grimaces. It was not time to "do" anything, but I used my own posture to ground my own energy field and to provide a stable force field near her. Then, just when I sensed in my own body that her writhing was becoming unbearable and she paused momentarily, I moved in on her. I knew that her coiling hands were closest to me and I could engage them quickly. I had to place clear pressure against her palms so she could feel me, but in such a way that the contact would be at the edge of her space and not too close to her center. Together, we created a strong boundary to mediate the point of contact. By pressing with increasing strength against her hands, I could sense her and she sensed me. I had to close my eyes to concentrate fully on the feeling between our hands, otherwise I felt I would be seduced into the chaotic and angry distraction of her other movements and angry eyes. She felt like my hissing cat or a mad Medusa. I could not look too directly into her eyes, but kept my awareness of the steady point of contact between us. As I pushed against her, her inward-pulling energy began to mobilize and focus on my push. It described a figure eight as it spiraled in toward her center, then looped back around toward our point of contact. As she pushed me with increasing strength, her whole body got behind the push, and soon both our centers were engaged in the relationship. Once her breathing and "gut" center were engaged, a feeling level came into our relationship. I felt her direct her anger and frustration at me, while I kept my push steady and neutral. Her push escalated until it peaked with a shriek.

After that, the quality of the relationship changed dramatically. P threw herself sideways across my lap, letting her whole torso touch me. I could lean over her back, with no interference from moving body parts, and use the whole of my own torso to contain her. She was like a child twitching in my lap, asking for strong cradling. I circled her with my arm while I held her tightly and steadily, protecting her new vulnerability. Feeling safe within the confines of my human straitjacket, she was able to soften and quiet down. When her agitated, endless movements were contained, phrased, and came to closure, then she could thank me.

If the elements described in this session were taken metaphorically instead of as concrete movement, how could the metaphors describe and illuminate processes of a verbal psychotherapy session? I will focus on two aspects of a psychotherapy session: (1) the movements and nonverbal communication that are part of any interaction and that indicate intra- and interpersonal dynamics, and (2) elements of energy, space, and composition that make up style of rhetoric. Further, physical dimensions of movement, such as containing and holding, metaphorically speak about patterns in a therapeutic interaction. How, then, can these movement elements appear in a verbal psychotherapy session?

1. Body. Taken as a form, the body of any client yields important diagnostic information about the personality. Is it fragmented, organized, flaccid, or taut? Is there a central organizing support? How do the parts fit together? Implicit in this diagnostic is an assumption that "you are your body"; that is, the body reflects personality style and ego strengths. Further, "body" may refer to the body of speech. Is the language fragmented or organized; are there central support themes; how do the parts hang together? Finally, body may refer also to the body of the therapist. Does the therapist have a strong observing ego (spine) to ground and contain the client's diffusion? What imaginal and subtle body shifts does a therapist do with her body during the session to provide a good holding environment for the client?

2. Space. Looked at as a composition, the spatial configurations of the mover in space is also an important diagnostic tool. Translated into a psychotherapy session, we might notice whether the client places himself in a corner, close or far from the leader. Does he feel that he must take up just a little spot; can he sprawl, be close to others? Does he tend to shrink into the background or thrust into the foreground?

The kinaesphere of a client may be visible as soon as she enters the room. Does she take up a lot of room; is she expansive; are the gestures large or small? In her rhetoric, is she expansive or constricted; are the sentences full or terse? How much of the conversational space does she occupy, and will she accommodate in size to coordinate with a listener?

Boundaries are one of the most salient dimensions for the borderline client. This may be felt as soon as a client enters the room. There may be a sense of awkwardness in passing each other, in glances or gestures that linger slightly too long, in a feeling of sticking to each other. The body might not have a clear definition, and there might be a sense of emotions spilling out. Words might also spill out and lack containment or tension. Both therapist and client may experience a sense of being flooded by sensations and affect, without an appropriate screening mechanism. The session might run over just a few extra minutes.

Fuzzy boundaries obviously affect the relationships one can make with objects in space. In the opening example, the client had difficulty making clear paths through space toward others in the room. Because she could not establish clear movement boundaries and because her boundaries were masked by chaotic movement "clutter," she could not establish definite contact at the boundary. Her relationships were diffuse and unclear. With movements that spiraled back toward her own center rather than outward, her relationships were self-absorbed.

Negative space refers to the space around or through solid forms. This may be observed in actual movement; for example, the client in this example did not make an active relationship to the space around her body. Space may also mean the space around thoughts or words in conversation. Another borderline client observed that she was characteristically overwhelmed by feelings and could not "step back" from them or get any space around them. She also identified too readily and felt others' pain as her own; she could not separate and find space between another and herself. She would either merge or withdraw and could not find an interplay. Movements and emotions dance in the context of reciprocal space; without this spatial context, they are over-whelming or out of proportion. Finally, space can de-scribe the therapist's "technical neutrality" (Kernberg, 1984, p. 103) of maintaining a distance from the pa-tient's intrapsychic conflicts. Without it, the therapist is sucked into strong primitive defenses.

Space can also be experienced as open territory in which we set roadmaps. P clearly indicated to everyone else in the room that she could not tolerate a direct fron-tal approach, but might allow a sideways, indirect one. As a metaphor, this might indicate that a verbal state-ment should not be too confrontational, but must be more indirect. In some forms of therapy, the therapist will sit at the side of the patient rather than in front. If eye contact is made, it might be better to look from the corner of the eye than to look too straightforwardly.

3. Energy. Words and thoughts, as well as actions, can be quick or slow, light or heavy, tense or free. In a session, a therapist can sense the qualities of energy of the communication and can use this sense to clarify therapeutic issues. Time, one of the elements of energy, describes not only quick or slow but also the phrasing of the movements. If the movements were read as a mu-sical score, then the individual qualitative notes would cluster in phrases. These phrases would be strung to-gether to create a lyrical line in which the bits of musi-cal information are organized into coherent temporal units. P did not group her movements so that they came to either closure or impact; they seemed to go on and on. Similarly, a client's voice may lack phrasing or im-pact, and the therapeutic issues might be about lack of assertiveness or effectiveness in life. In a verbal ses-sion, attending not only to what and how things are

said but also reading between the lines of how these things are put together, yields important information about how the client organizes his or her world.

Interaction

When I saw P as my cat, I remembered that it took 6 years before my cat let me touch her. She taught me a great deal about patience. P and I met each other animal-self to animal-self, in a nonverbal language of trust-building. Thinking about our relationship in the imagery of animals dancing together rather than in the mechanistic imagery of "objects" and "relationships" reminded me of the activity in the *Little Prince* called "apprivoiser," or "to tame." In this story, the wild fox teaches the young prince how to approach and quiet him so that they are able to be present together. In my story with P, I had to sense how to approach her, maintain safety, and help her wild energy transform itself into peace.

In terms of movement and choreography, I used my energy to contain and transform a process. I began by sitting very still and concentrating on stabilizing and grounding myself in order to provide a feeling of holding at a safe distance. I was actually imaging support and containment to help bring image and movement together. As I sensed some openness in her, I came closer. By creating a boundary and pushing against it, I was communicating that I was present, but setting and clarifying limits. This allowed her to feel safe enough to express her energy; it went from "impress" to "express," and moved outward toward relationship with another person. As I held my push steady, I could feel her energy implode inward, and I kept myself present as a steady force, inviting contact but not violating her trust or invading her. She used my holding to integrate and mobilize herself.

When she screamed, I sensed her new vulnerability. She seemed to be asking me to mother her, to hold and cradle her. Yet her twitching body asked for a firm grasp, a tough love that she could feel and trust. She was asking whether I could handle her, could hold all that turmoil. She let me hold her with my torso; our relationship went from peripheral (hands) to central (center of gravity, guts, emotions).

The healing happened because I deliberately used my energy as a "holding object" to help her silent regression take place. As a re-mother with whom she was experiencing trust, I held her child's fragmented self and let her project her turmoil onto me and then helped her reintegrate using my own self. Through my active setting of boundaries and use of presence, she was able to experience a moment of congruence between inner and outer self, and we were able to experience an integrated relationship together. Finally, compositionally, our session had the form of a good choreography—a clear beginning, middle, and end. Suzanne Langer (1953) claims that art creates patterns that organize emotional energy; our A–B–A form gave coherence and closure to P's unbearable chaos.

These elements of dance and choreography—use of presence, energy, body, space, and form—are present in any healing therapeutic encounter. A sensitive therapist would use his presence and timing to guide the flow of the session. It is important to say, however, that dancers begin with a natural sensitivity, but also receive special training in how to see. Dancers are trained to kinaesthetically feel, see, and improvise with spatial relationships, weight shifts, repetition, and mirroring of movement themes, boundaries, and rhythm. Like visual artists, dancers are trained in an aesthetic mode of perception that has elements in common with other arts, but which also has its unique kinaesthetic dimension. This language, which articulates forms of process, can be helpful in describing the process of the therapeutic dance.

Patient and Psychotherapist: The Music
Alice Shields

As both psychotherapist and composer, I have felt myself drawn to viewing each role through eyes and ears sharpened by the other. I believe that a sensitive understanding of some of the elements of musical composition can be of use to verbal psychotherapists as they create a session together with the patient as both music and the therapy session are related in that both display the expression of meaning and affect through the frame of time and the modality of sound. In fact, as many therapists are aware, the nonverbal—in our case, sound—components of the therapy session can often give more information about the patient's experience than the verbal content alone.

The Dramatic Dialogues Inherent in Thought and Music

[Music] arises from and expresses the structure of thought itself, with its multiplicity of figures and viewpoints, and its lifelong conversations (Watkins, 1986).

I have taken the liberty of preceding this quote with the word "music" in place of what Watkins actually wrote, which is "drama," for it seems to me that music, or any art, is based on the essentially dialogic nature of thought. And that the dialogic nature of our thought is based on vague or more well-defined imaginal others inside ourselves, these imaginal others themselves being activated by the original dialogue between ourselves as infants and our mothers.

It seems further that the origin of the dialogue in the mother–infant interaction may also be assisted, as Melanie Klein suggested, by the splitting of good and bad part-objects during the earliest period of the infant's experience, the paranoid-schizoid position. Klein, as interpreted by Segal, says:

> One of the achievements of the paranoid–schizoid position is splitting...which allows the ego to emerge out of chaos and to order its experiences (Segal, 1973).

I would suggest that the recognition and then the projection of the bad object (or later, its repression) is what Jung referred to as the Shadow, and that as therapists part of our function is to help the patient become aware of their internal Shadow, the complement of verbal expressions and nonverbal, sound expressions.

First the patient's imaginal others have to be defined, one at a time, in sensory sound characteristic of their modes of expression, establishing recognizable sound traits—e.g., in vocal timbre or melodic intonation patterns as in questioning, ascending intonation as opposed to descending, commanding ones. Recently I asked a young classical musician patient to describe his bodily experience of fear when he performed in public, which was the reason he was seeking my help. He described a cold wind rising from his feet to his ribs, which would be followed by his experience of his lower body decomposing. I asked him to imitate that cold wind with his voice: He made a long whooshing sound. After discussing how it felt to make this sound, we decided to try it on his instrument (a wind instrument). He blew into it, creating a complex sound, kind of like a train whistle, which he crescendoed and decrescendoed on. At the beginning of this session he had felt the "whoosh" as something alien to him, as something attacking him from without. As he "became" the dreaded "whoosh" by controlling or expressing it through his wind instrument, he gained a measure of refinement of one of the imaginal others within himself (or a measure of integration, if you prefer), an accomplishment that allowed him on his next public performance to feel much less debilitation from this formerly intrusive image.

Once the patient's imaginal others have emerged in some sound detail by themselves, the further interactions (counterpoint, in music) of each figure with the narrating personality and with the other imaginal personalities can open up complexities in each character's sounds, revealing conflicts or opposing aspects of a character. These stresses within the character are sometimes heard in the therapy session as heightened affect; e.g., the voice's abrupt changes in amplitude (loudness) and jagged melodic intonation, as in anger. Sometimes the character remains incarnated in sound with opposing characteristics—heard as changes in the musical parameters of the voice—and at other times the character splits in two, one part being the complement of the other as can be developed in the sound–vocal characteristic of the two.

CHAPTER 2

Thematic Form in Therapy and Music

Before the patient's imaginal others and their expression through the sounds of the patient can begin to be defined, however, it is often useful for the therapist (and the patient) to look at the thematic material in a session, as these often indicate some incipient struggles in the patient to define himself.

Rarely discussed in the training of psychotherapists is the literal form in time that the dialogue between patient and psychotherapist takes. Of course, the most obvious similarity between a therapy session and piece of music is that both occur within the framework of time. The therapy session is generally under one hour in length, whereas a piece of music may be a few minutes or many hours long. Both may consist within the time frame of similar structures of organized material. Organized thematic material may be seen in music as repeated (or sometimes, always changing and never repeated) melodic phrases, which may find analogy in the therapy session in the repeated concerns of the patient or the therapist.

Rondo Form

Just one among many melodic forms in music, which is often found in the therapy session, is "rondo" form: "abacada," in which each letter represents a certain melody with, in the case of rondo form, the "a" melody repeating between other melodies, which are not repeated. This musical form may be experienced in the therapy session as the patient or therapist returning to a certain concern, feeling, or thought, alternating with new material. Whether it is the patient or the therapist who creates the returning "a" event is important for the understanding of the psychodynamics of the session: If the "a" material is inserted by the therapist, the session may have an insistent, perhaps confronting, or even intrusive character to the patient, depending on the degree of relatedness of the new theme. On the other hand, if the "a" material is brought up by the patient, the repeated material can be seen as representative of the patient's present state of being in which the repeat of the "a" material indicates an attempt at mastery and integration or, at worst, of obsession defenses at work.

ABA Form

Another common form in music and therapy can be described as "aba," a tripartite form in which the material first brought up returns after an excursion into other matters. This structure in psychotherapy is often formed by the therapist in a summing up of the session. However, the patient may create this form, perhaps indicating an introjection of the therapist or a strengthening of the ego.

Theme and Variations Form

A musical form seen with certain types of patients (just which patients will I hope become clear later) is that of theme and variations, or "$a^1a^2a^3a^4a^5$," represented in the therapy session by partial repetitions and enlargements upon the initial concern. Thus, the therapist may introduce an interpretation of what the patient has just said and the patient may vary the therapist's variation, staying on the main theme nevertheless.

If the theme and variations form is desired by the therapist and the patient does not either repeat or vary the therapist's interpretation but turns to new material, the rest of the session may, if the patient is not made too anxious by the "a" material, take one of the previously discussed forms. If the patient *is* made very anxious by the "a" material, the following form may result.

Through-Composed Form

The "through-composed" form, or "abcdef," may indicate the avoidance of an uncomfortable feeling, or anxiety. Sometimes the resistance to working on a concern—seen as the absence of repetition—may be conscious, in which case the therapist may wish to draw the patient's attention to the avoidance of structure in the session. At other times, the through-composed form may indicate overwhelming anxiety and the therapist may choose to create a containing structure with repetition of one or more themes of the patient.

Repetition–Mirroring versus Counterpoint–Confrontation

In general, repetitions with slight differences from the patient's communications are known as mirroring, with interpretations as variations on the theme.

It is important to remember that it is not just the ideational communications of the patient that are expressed in the above forms and can therefore be repeated or varied (mirrored or interpreted) by the therapist (although the ideational theme are easier to grasp, it *seems*), but often the nonverbal sound expressions, such as vocal timbre, speech rhythm and speed, loudness characteristics, and melodic intonation.

As therapists, we can gather that there are three different types of sound–time responses to a patient's communication (Gendlin, 1981).

1. Repetition of theme
2. Variation of theme
3. Counterpoint (confrontation, or different theme)

The Personality Types and Their Experience of Time

It seems that we can distinguish among people four different organizational experiences of time, corresponding to Jung's four basic personality types: thinking, feeling, sensation, and intuition (Mann, Siegler, and Osmond, 1972). I would first like to link Jung's two evaluating types—thinking and feeling—with two psychoanalytic categories (in pathology): the obsessive–schizoid and the hysteric–depressive.

Keeping this comparison in mind, I will discuss the four Jungian types' experience of time and their implications for therapy.

Thinking Type: Linear Time

The thinking type, often seen in pathology as obsessive or schizoid, experiences the important quality of time in the therapy sessions as linear, related to the time line, with no particular importance placed on past, present, *or* future, but only on the flow forward (see Mann *et al.*, 1972, on which I heavily draw). The thinking type's experience may be most closely mirrored in the therapist's summation of the session by the latter not lingering on any *one* theme in the session, but on a recounting of the development of themes throughout the session, on the flow itself.

Further experience of material in the session — say, *present* relationships (including that with the therapist) — will be felt with the strongest rapport by the patient if no *one* of the past or present or future ramifications of the patient's situation is exclusively discussed, but will be felt at its strongest if the time line (the relationship of all three dimensions of linear time to the patient's discussion) are clarified.

The Feeling Type: Cyclic Time and Relating to the Past

The therapist who wishes to enhance the feeling type's experience of being understood will relate present experiences to the patient's past emotional experiences; the therapist will often create rondo or theme and variations forms in conjunction with the patient. The feeling type's preference for a particular thematic form often is expressed by repetition.

The shadow element of the feeling type's orientation to time is often the lack of directed, future possibilities of experiences from the past. Thus, the feeling type often can expand his or her experience to a linear, time-line-oriented approach to possibilities whereas the thinking type often needs to grow in the direction of intensification of feeling tone in both past and present experience. In other words, the feeling type needs to develop a more "active" orientation to use Deikman's term (Deikman, 1973), and the thinking type a more "receptive" one. As Deikman mentions, it is the action mode of consciousness that is most typical of Western

European–American culture, and this preference—usually quite out of awareness—is often expressed by therapists covertly with their patients, *all* patients, regardless of the personality type's *own* preferred interpretation of linear, cyclic (reference to the past), present moment, or future modes of time perception. Thus, there is often in therapy a mismatch, a lack of understanding of the patient's reality due to the therapist's not being aware, first of all, of his or her particular relationship to the experience of time.

The Sensation Type: Existing in the Present

Concerned with the sensory perception of what is immediate, the sensation type's experience of time is most closely mirrored by the therapist relating not to past causes or future possibilities of the patient's behavior and inner state but responding to and drawing out further the details of the patient's sensory (perhaps sound) expressions *as they occur* in the present. Once the patient's perception of what is important in his or her time experience has been mirrored, the therapist may help the patient to grow in perception of the other dimensions of time and the organization of experience, helping the patient to experience with affect the past causes and future possibilities of behavior and inner states.

With the sensation type it can often be productive of growth for the therapist to point out the time line in the session and any recurrences of themes. It can be often useful, depending on the patient's ego strengths, to enlarge upon (i.e., develop in great sensory detail) the exact nature of two different themes; in other words, help clarify for the patient the aversive feeling from the positive (splitting), and thereby to aid awareness of the different imaginal figures within the patient.

The Intuitive Type: Relating to the Future

The person with intuition dominant is the type least related to the past or present experience of life in general and in the therapy session: He or she tends to focus consciousness only on the possibilities of an experience, often without much affect. In more pathological states, where the intuitive person has very little access to the time relationships of the other three personality types, the patient has little understanding of causal relationships (linear perception of time). This lack of grounding in past or present experience—or rather the intuitive patient's preference for interpreting "reality" in terms of aggregates, of whole patterns or gestalts—can often create in the session through-composed, nonrepetitive form. The therapist (who, of course, is usually in our culture listening for causal links in linear time) may perceive the intuitive patient as jumping from theme to theme and may then help the patient to trace the associative links between two of these seemingly disconnected themes. Often the themes can be linked to inner imaginal figures, each having a different viewpoint. And often the intuitive's abrupt leaps in theme will occur because of a lack of clear dialogue between the inner characters, resulting in abrupt shifts of character, much as if in a room full of people everyone were one at a time desperately grabbing attention, afraid that if they made a more gradual or smooth entrance they wouldn't be listened to. I am saying, then, that a full affectual and imaged experience of the theme (subpersonality) in the session, including the making conscious of the unconscious transitions between themes ("flow" or gradual transition), can assist the intuitive patient, who indeed is in other ways eager to experience the future, to develop into also feeling the importance of past and present experience in his or her anticipation of the future.

Units of Sound Perception in Time

The "Present Moment" and the Phonemic Clause

Let's consider for a moment some perceived units of sound, starting with the smallest. According to the psychologist Clynes (1977), the smallest—i.e., the *shortest*—unit of time in which we can perceive sound is about .2 second. This "present moment" represents the length of time necessary for us to hear a spoken syllable (or a short note in music). These smallest units of perception and articulation are linked together in speech in groups of 7 or 8 syllables called phonemic clauses (Boomer, 1978), whose sound features are voice pitch, rhythm, and loudness. It is my belief that it is the phonemic clause that carries the sentic form (Clynes, 1977, discussed later), the varieties of which phylogenetically express emotion, and thus carry the particular nonverbally expressed affect of the patient, through his or her voice, to the therapist.

I would like to compare the verbal phonemic clause with the melodic motif in music—often of only one or two or three pitch intervals—around which a longer, fuller melody is often constructed. I believe that the phonemic clause and the melodic motif, both related in their significant melodic character, are the elementary sound units carrying the general nature of the conflictual situation to be projected upon this melodic material by the listener (Shields & Robbins, 1980).

The smallest perceived sound units then can be said to be syllables, which in turn are "chunked" into aggregates of 7 or 8 syllables in the phonemic clause, which itself carries (partly through learned musical style in a particular culture) nonverbally understood information as to the speaker's present state (conscious or unconscious). The timbre of the speaker's voice, e.g., rich or hollow, will carry the nonverbally perceived information as to the exact nature of the affectual conflict expressed by the melodic contour of the phonemic clause (Shields & Robbins, 1980).

Organization of Time Units into Themes

Further organization, or chunking, of units in time (rhythms) has been noted by Lomax (1982) in music from many cultures, the typical durations lasting from 10 seconds to 10 minutes. These durations are similar in my view to the lengths of nonverbal sound communications in the therapy session, with the shorter durations usually indicating the presence of resistance or anxiety. It is interesting to note that melodies often last for at least 10 seconds in music and can be repeated or varied for much longer. (I have found, in my own music experience, that a 10-minute-long piece can be written, or someone else's listened to, with much more ease than a longer piece in which multiple complexities seem to enter.)

It seems to me that the units of only 10 second's duration in sound are more likely to be nonverbal ones, perhaps heard in vocal timbre or speech tempo. *Verbal* themes of this short duration would immediately alert the therapist to a perhaps critical state on the part of the patient. Thus, it seems as if in most conversation between individuals in a noncritical state there are unconscious tendencies to express different themes or ideas in a certain duration, the exact length of which is determined by the social situation. In the therapy situation, the maximum duration of many of the themes discussed (in the Thematic Form in Therapy and Music section) often does not exceed 10 minutes. The implications of longer duration are too wide to go into here.

Synchrony and Asynchrony: Sound and Movement in the Patient

When a phonemic clause or a word is sounded, the body of the speaker moves in response, at a delay of 50 milliseconds to 1 second (Condon, 1982). The listener's body will move also in response to the word heard. Thus, we entrain our bodies and lock in, even with inanimate sounds, within about 50 milliseconds. Normally the body will hold quietly or move slowly on a consonant and speed up on a vowel. Psychopathology is often revealed in a patient in his or her lack of movement on hearing or saying vowels, or the displacement of the movement in time; in others words, to a nonculturally sanctioned part of speech.

The experience of "flow" in the therapy session is usually related to this rhythmical "dance" between both participants as they make sounds and move to their own sounds as well as to the other's. Any stopping in this rhythmic flow of sound and motion is experienced as semiotic, indicative of some intrusive element.

Jaffe and Anderson (1979) speculate that conversation grows out of the rhythmic interaction between mother and infant. Further, it has been claimed that the nature of the mother's vocalization and movements with the baby is often repetitive, with minor variations, and that it is through her repetitiveness that the infant learns to predict her next move. The infant's prediction of the mother's next sound can be seen in all non-coactive or turn-taking (dialogic) vocalizations in which both mother and infant match duration of behavior–pause cycles. In the adult interaction in therapy, phrase-duration matching between patient and therapist is a sign of rapport experienced by both, whereas wide variance of phrase-duration between patient and therapist is experienced as lack of flow or rapport.

In line with Watkins' view (1986) mentioned above of the dramatic, dialogic nature of thought, it appears to me that the occurrence of sound–movement synchrony in the patient may indicate the (unconsciously experienced by the patient) presence of an imaginal other struggling to express itself to the conscious personality. Thus, one way of establishing synchrony in the session would be to encourage this imaginal other to express itself, perhaps making the sounds and movements that express its personality. In encouraging such a previously intrusive figure to express itself, it is often helpful to also define the character of the narrating ego (the part of the self consciously identified with) in the sounds (and words) and movements that best express *its* nature.

The Defenses as Heard in the Patient's Voice

It seems that on hearing any sound, but especially vocal sound, the listener's larynx is entrained, that is, takes the same muscular position, as the speaker's or singer's (Moses, 1954). Thus, the listener's larynx assumes the physical position to make those very sounds he or she is hearing. The therapist can, by listening to the nonverbal sound quality of the patient's voice, feel in herself the patient's physical sensations and the emotions such a body state bring up.

The Obsessive Defense in the Voice

If a patient's voice is tensely held in a very limited pitch range (analogous in the larynx to tightening any other muscle, such as the anus in obsessives) and the timbre is restricted in octave overtones (often resulting in a somewhat "nasal" effect with little resonance or vibration in the sinuses and a feeling of tension and lack of openness in the nasopharynx) it is probable that the patient is using obsessive or schizoid defenses. This diagnosis can be hypothesized in the beginning of the initial session through—if the therapist's ear is not highly developed—feeling in one's larynx the emotional state of the patient, thus guiding one's history taking and approach to the patient.

Often people with obsessive defenses will force their voice to stay in one narrow pitch area, often the medium range of pitches possible for their voice. As the relationship between patient and therapist progresses and the patient seems ready to accept some repressed feelings, the expressive (or other) therapist may suggest that the patient experiment with letting his or her voice go into a different pitch area. If the patient chooses a high, loud pitch, one might assume an attempt to express aggressive or sexual feelings, whereas a high, soft pitch might indicate an identification or characterization of the patient as a child; or, in a man's case, an identification with a woman or with a female imaginal other.

Low, loud sounds may indicate the presence of sensual feelings or aggressiveness of not quite so pressing a kind as the high, low sound discussed above. For a woman, a low, loud sound sometimes indicates, if it is unvarying, an avoidance of vulnerability and possibly an identification as a man.

Low, soft sounds, if expressed in a timbre weak in overtones (formants), usually indicate depression. A low, soft sound *rich* in timbre generally indicates warm, loving feelings.

The Hysteric Defense in the Voice

The patient who presents a melodic or intonational profile of very wide pitch range is at the other end of the emotional spectrum from the obsessive person discussed above. This very wide-ranging (and usually fast) speech pattern may indicate a fragile ego in danger of being overwhelmed by the unconscious, or Shadow. The patient in such a state can sometimes be encouraged to slow the speed of speech and reduce the melodic range.

The experience of a greater feeling of control, which increased tension in the vocal and breathing muscles can temporarily give the person of fragile ego and obsessive defense, can be heard in the patient's voice as a comparatively more restricted pitch range. But in general I believe it preferable to hear what that original, wide-ranging voice wants to say. As with any intense expression of human feeling, this is easier to do within a frame, a holding container. One such frame, the time frame of the therapy session, may be enough of a holding environment for some people. For others, I find that expression of such intense feeling within another ritual, that of artistic expression, offers a more secure, holding environment. (See Shields & Robbins, 1980, for an intensive discussion of the two extremes of timbre heard in the voice of the patient; that is, "head" and "chest" voice.)

Typically, the hysterical–depressive patient avoids the louder vocal sounds, thus indicating an avoidance of hostility and intense sexual feeling. The characteristic, more repressed hysterical timbre is high and soft, resembling a child's voice, in both sexes.

The two categories of hysteric and obsessive in the above section might just as well have been termed [after Deikman (1973) according to the two modes of consciousness for most human beings] the active and the receptive, which have contrasting ways of dealing with experience: either through focused attention and therefore muscular and sound rigidity when seen in pathology, or through peripheral perception—in pathology the giving up of control—resulting in muscular flaccidity and exaggerated sound expression. Each type, active–obsessive and receptive–hysteric, has its own basic and preferred organization of the experience of time, as discussed above, which can be called lineal and nonlineal or cyclic (Lee, 1973).

How Emotion Is Conveyed in Sound

At times we seem to know, in listening both to patients and to music, that a specific emotion is being expressed. It seems obvious that this emotion is being carried by some nonverbal parameter of sound, for it often happens that we pick up a feeling from the non-verbal sound that is at variance with what is being expressed by the words alone. Clynes (1977, 1982) offers as an answer to this age-old question of how emotion is expressed in sound his empirical studies of certain temporal sensory patterns, which he calls sentic forms, each of which is associated with a certain emotional state.

Clynes (1977) describes seven sentic forms of emotional expression. I find these to be roughly divisible into two categories: abrupt versus gradual parameter changes. Emotions are further recognized within the abrupt or gradual categories by differing in their specific attack, duration, and decay characteristics. Emotions expressing positive connectivity, such as love, reverence, and grief, are expressed in sound by *gradual* parameter changes in melody, amplitude, and rhythm. Emotions expressing separateness, such as anger and hate, are expressed through *abrupt* changes in sound parameters.

In Clyne's view, "blocking," or deadened, repressed feeling, results when a sentic form is not allowed to complete itself. Blocking can be considered the equivalent of ambivalence. What is typical of ambivalence is the attempt to express two conflicting emotions at the same time. Thus the result is noncompletion of any sentic form and an inner experience of unclear affect. A recent Jungian technique to deal with this situation is to encourage the clarification of one's imaginal others in their contrasting sensory expression. When a single imaginal other is communicating, its particular sentic form tends to be realized more fully.

A Final Word about Music and Therapy

Music (and the sounds of a patient's speech), being basically nonverbal, is automatically more ambiguous than spoken or written language, and thus allows the projection of a certain type of conflictual situation upon it (Shields and Robbins, 1980). Further, music and the nonverbal sounds in speech establish the specific character of the projected conflict through the redundancies found in sound, through coherent and mutually supportive expression of this *one* projected conflict in the sound parameters of melody, dynamics, timbre, and so on. It is when all these sound parameters are appropriate to the relationship implied by the melodic line that we say a piece of music, regardless of style or culture, has integrity or is *integrated*.

As part of the process of integration in music, we might expect that each parameter would express the sentic form desired; that this one sentic form would be expressed in every parameter of the music. As an analogy to this maintenance of a certain sentic form in all the parameters of a piece of music (as long as perhaps 10 seconds to 10 minutes or more), I put forth that this process can be regarded in both music and therapy as the detailed experience of an imaginary being in oneself projected upon the music.

The same holds true regarding integrity in the patient's verbal and nonverbal sound expressions: If all the nonverbal sounds work to enhance and clarify through the appropriate sentic form the verbal statement, then we say that the patient is "in touch" with herself or is not conflicted. In other words, the patient is expressing in both the verbal and nonverbal modalities of sound one particular state of being, or imaginal other.

When we hear a piece of music in which there is no clear establishment of mood or feeling, we see that the parameters of that piece are either not expressing complete sentic forms (or, more rarely, conflicting sentic forms of different shapes). Much music composed in any period is not clear in its feeling, and thus does not touch us as deeply as does what we call "great" or more redundant music where the various parameters are expressing the same sentic form.

The analogue of music without this integrity is what we see so often in patients and indeed in most so-called "normal" people: incomplete or conflicting expression of sentic form. Thus, the patient who complains of boredom often has incomplete expression of sentic forms in his melodic intonation in speech: This is often heard as lack of rise and fall in the intonation of the voice, pointing to repression of more intense feelings. This obviously resembles our description of the rigidification expressed by the obsessive. The hysteric often does not express complete sentic forms either, but a generalized state of excitement lacking the clear shapes that seem to intensify our experiencing of emotion.

In both music and therapy, it seems necessary to express *one* sentic form in our sound expressions at a time; that is, to clarify which part of us is speaking now, and to let this part speak fully and intensely in the melody of our voices, in the loudness or softness, the fastness or slowness, the dramatic or the mellow timbre. In the final analysis, it seems that there is a conclusion to be drawn: At least as far as I can see, what is good aesthetically—in music, and perhaps in all the arts—is good psychotherapeutically.

The Theatrical Dimensions of Psychotherapy
David Read Johnson

For years psychoanalysts and psychotherapists have studied drama and theater as psychological events. They have concluded that indeed drama is a psychological event and that under certain conditions it is even psychotherapeutic. The field of drama therapy has emerged from this exploration (Landy, 1986). But in this chapter I will ask: Is psychotherapy a dramatic or theatrical event? Does psychotherapy fulfill the aesthetic standards of the theater? I will ask this despite the fact that Freud thought this proposal was at heart "a repudiation of analysis, even though it is disguised in a friendly, indeed in too flattering a manner" (Freud, 1920, p. 191). Clearly, psychotherapy is not theater, but might have theatrical elements. To discover this we need to know what the essential elements of theater are.

Theater

What is theater? Of what does it consist? While to those in the theater world this is a complex question addressed to innumerable books, monographs, and manifestos, to everyone else it is a relatively simple question. Perhaps it is best to think simply. First, theater takes place in a special *space* and at a special *time*, set off from ordinary life in some manner. One *goes to* the theater, it does not emerge fluidly from everyday interactions. Second, theater is the enactment of a *story*, usually written by a playwright but sometimes produced spontaneously by the actors. Third, the story is reenacted by *actors* who pretend to be the characters. Fourth, theater requires an *audience*, who observe the action and temporarily suspend their disbelief in the pretense. Fifth, drama means the experiencing and purging of pent-up emotion, through laughter or sadness, in a process referred to as *catharsis*. Let us examine each of these elements to see how they appear in psychodynamically oriented psychotherapy.

The Stage Space

Theater occurs in a space set off from everyday life. It is a symbol for the sacred space in which contact is made with the spirits of the otherworld, originally by shamans or priests, and now by actors accessing imaginative realms. As David Cole (1975) writes, "Stage space is the physicalization of the actor's apartness...the spatial symptom of the psychic gap which one who serves noumena opens out between the rest of us and himself" (p. 94). This gap or boundary refers to the distinction between realms of experience: between the present and the past, between ordinary life and the world of archetypal myth. As the lights go down, we descend into darkness, into night, into dream, and the veil/curtain is pulled aside, and we enter through the portal of the proscenium arch into the imaginative world, which Cole refers to as the *illud tempus*. One participates in this theater with a mixture of reverence, curiosity, and the suspension of disbelief. One prepares to experience the characters, not the actors; the drama, not the director's blocking.

Psychotherapy also occurs in a special space, one in which the boundary between everyday life and therapeutic life is strictly drawn. It too is modeled on the boundary around the sacred encounter, that of supplicant and priest. It too signals that what goes on in the therapy is a world apart.

Both of these spaces are transitional spaces (Winnicott, 1953) where fantasy and reality mix, and inner and outer worlds commune. As such they are creative spaces, satisfying what Rothenberg (1987) describes as the homospatial process underlying creativity: "actively conceiving two or more discrete entities occupying the same space, a conception leading to the articulation of new identities" (p. 7).

The Script

At the basis of the drama is a story, whether of tragic or comic dimensions, which the playwright attempts to articulate. In every story, so they say, there is the *hero*, representing the individual and his freedom, and there is *Fate*, representing the constraints to the hero's freedom: i.e., the world, the past, the gods, the group. It is the *tragic flaw* of the hero, as mortal being, which dooms him to this earth, like Sisyphus to his boulder, as a suffering (that it, conscious) being in the midst of a world not of his choosing. Regardless of the resolution of this struggle (e.g., death, forgiveness, acceptance, revolt, transcendence), the play is not the mere reiteration of an event, but makes reference to a level of inspiration, emotion, and unexpressed conflict that the audience has already experienced, but forgot. In this sense, a good story is both familiar and unfamiliar at the same time, that is, "uncanny" (Freud, 1919).

So what is the story in psychotherapy? Usually the client walks into the therapist's office with the story, or *a* story, and most therapists ask the client to tell them their story. But do they know their own story? Is it not true that the story which client and therapist seek is the *full* story, much of which the client is unaware? In fact the client comes into therapy wanting to know what the real story is, because he has been distressed by his own behavior that does not fit the story about himself he thinks he knows. In this sense, psychotherapy is a process of discovering the script that the client seems to be enacting, without knowing it. The therapist is a midwife to the real story, and the result of a full psychotherapy is a more explicit script of the past that gives meaning to the client's current behavior. As in most stories, the hero (the self) struggles against Fate (past traumas, circumstances of life beyond one's control). The ultimate recognition of the tragic flaw by the client comes with some pain (that motivated the forgetting of the story in the first place), and yet now leads to its resolution. Like Oedipus, the client sees that there is something awry, but blind to the story and blind to his own role in it, he seeks answers from his therapist, whom, like Tiresias, he initially ignores. Only later does he discover the truth. Even though that moment is one of pain and confusion, at the same time the realization/acceptance of the story dissolves the need to keep repeating it. Acknowledging Fate, one becomes free; confronting blindness, one learns to see.

Seeking the Character

Creating a role is the essential task of the actor, a process most developed by Stanislavski (1961). The basics of his system, now called the Method, include relaxation, focusing, the method of emotional memory, and the method of physical actions (Moore, 1974). His technique requires the actor to utilize his own inner emotions and prior experiences to infuse the character with emotional truthfulness. This contrasted with previous methods of actor training that were based purely on imitation of external mannerisms of characters.

Building a character begins with a period of relaxation and silence in which the actor, through introspection, concentrates on his inner state and his knowledge of the character in the context of the play (the given circumstances). Using the "Magic If"—that is, asking oneself: What would I do if I were in the situation of this character?—the actor accesses his own memories and emotions as a means of capturing the motivation of the character. The aim is to attach an inner feeling to each action; every gesture must reflect an inner experience. The intention, however, is always to bring life to the character, not the actor's own persona. "The actor must adjust himself to the role, not the role to himself" (Moore, 1974, p. 72). The actor, by understanding the intent of the playwright (the Superobjective), studying the details of the play (the given circumstances), and executing truthful physical actions, becomes a reincarnation of the character. By simultaneously maintaining both an inner awareness and truthful physical action the actor achieves what Stanislavski termed, public solitude.

Grotowski (1968) has extended Stanislavski's method through the concept of the poor theater. He views the essence of theater as "what happens between the actor and the spectator," so he deemphasizes or eliminates makeup, costumes, scenery, and even the script to focus on the actor as a vehicle for the illumination of collective myth. This parallels Freud's shift from hypnosis and other physical techniques to the bare encounter among therapist, patient, and unconscious. Grotowski trains the actor to allow unconscious forces that are even deeper than personal memory to emerge. His method is therefore one of the *via negativa*, not collecting skills, but removing personal blocks to the creative impulse.

> The ripening of the actor is expressed by a tension toward the extreme, by a complete stripping down, by the laying bare of one's own intimacy. The actor makes a total gift of himself...The result is freedom from the time-lapse between inner impulse and outer reaction in such a way that the impulse is already an outer reaction (Grotowski, 1968, p. 16).

When this is successful, the actor achieves a total act.

Cole (1975) uses the metaphor of psychic journey to describe the actor's task, comparing the actor to the shaman of tribal society who as a delegate from the audience seeks out the image in the otherworld *(illud tempus)*, and then returns with it. "The actor's first step in presenting the script *illud tempus* must likewise be a journey inward in search of those components of his own psychic life that coincide with the figures and events of the script *illud tempus*" (Cole, 1975, p. 10). In a process similar to possession, the actor achieves this contact with the otherworld, turns around, and returns to the audience, only now as the Character. This process of rounding occurs when the actor has been fully illuminated by the image of the character.

> I call this reversal in which the actor goes from masterful explorer to mastered vehicle the rounding. The rounding is the defining characteristics of theatrical performance. It is in the moment of the rounding that the theatre, as an event, is born (Cole, 1975, p. 15).

Can we locate the reincarnation, the total act, the rounding, in psychotherapy? Indeed, what are the roles? When the client comes into the office, he has been enacting a role in a story he is not fully aware of. His neurotic behavior speaks to some other presence which has possessed him, and is causing some discomfort. In this sense he has the opposite problem of the characters in Pirandello's *Six Characters in Search of an Author*, who want to get back in the play. He is a person wanting to get out of one. The purpose of therapy is to discover who his role is and free him from compulsively reenacting it. Unlike people, these unconscious patterns of behavior, or internal characters, do not change. As one of Pirandello's characters exclaims,

> That is the very difference! Our reality doesn't change: it can't change! It can't be other than what it is, because it is already fixed for ever. It's terrible. Ours is an immutable reality which should make you shudder (Pirandello, 1952, p. 266)

This immutability is shared by all the inhabitants of the *illud tempus*.

Clearly the relationship between client and therapist departs from normal social interaction. The professional relationship demands different behaviors on both parties than in effect can be viewed as roles. The therapist remains responsive, positive, warm, neutral in judgment, and does not share personal conflicts. The client is asked to talk a lot and describe inner feelings no matter how embarrassing, including feelings about the therapist. This process is designed to facilitate the exploration of the internal world, where important characters lay. In a process similar to that of the actor attempting to build a character—relaxation, concentration, and emotional memory—various images are called up. As the therapy progresses, both therapist and client begin to build a picture of these various characters, and through the transference the therapist is perceived, and experiences, aspects of these characters. That is, the otherwise real relationship between them is transformed into another that is reminiscent of earlier ones in the patient's life. Thus, they begin to take on their roles.

> Transference is a universal dramatic phenomenon. Without the ability to transfer past to present, actuality to symbol, the individual would exist in a drab, unidimensional world where play and drama are nonexistent and all things are as they seem (Landy, 1986, p. 96)

The therapist's interventions at this stage are intended to facilitate this process, to deepen the client's experience of the new roles. At some point, the client "rounds" on his inner characters and the transference emerges full force in the session.

Both real and transference relationships coexist, just as the relationship between two actors coexists with that between their two characters. But as the therapy progresses the contrast between these two relationships increases. Often the beginning of a session is filled with slightly uncomfortable small talk between the two "people" about the weather, bills, or scheduling. As they sit down and a silence falls, however, it might as well be the lights dimming before the curtain opens on a different relationship, one evoked by the "script" of the patient's internal world.

I am reminded of a play that a friend of mine was in. He was thrilled to have a part in a low-budget, off-off Broadway play. During the performance, as he was exiting from an intensely emotional scene, the stage wall near him began to fall over. He of course stopped his exit and tried to hold it up, while maintaining character. This was an obvious strain on him, however, and when the wall finally did fall down, he broke out into a laugh. The stage illusion had been shattered.

Similarly, while in my office after a year of treatment, a client was describing her great respect for me, and I was trying to relate her feelings about me to those toward her father. She didn't see the connection. The moment was quite intense. All of a sudden, the shade on the window fell down. The sun was now shining directly into her eyes, so I had to fix it. Unfortunately, it was on a high window, and the only way I could change it was to put a chair on my desk and climb onto it while she supported the chair, since it was wobbly. The shade kept coming off the hook, and precious time in her session was being taken up by my awkwardness. At first we didn't laugh. After failing to get the shade up, I returned to my chair, smiled, and said,"Now what were you saying about your father?" and she said, squinting in the direct sunlight, "You know, you're right, I was talking about *him*" and we both shared a hearty laugh. She had clearly experienced the illusion of the transference.

Most therapists know the terrible disjunction that occurs when the transferential relationship is intruded upon by the ordinary, "real" relationship.

The Audience

Various dramatists have defined the audience's function differently, though all agree that the spectator is a full participant in the act of theater. The audience can at times function as the receptive experiencer of the emotions raised in the play, or, alternatively, can be placed in the position of the witness or judge of the actions on stage. The power of theater can be derived from the cathartic effect of immersing oneself in the action, or by the vicarious thrill of witnessing the actor's exhibition and confession of extreme acts. Thus, excitement can be generated both by increasing and by decreasing the audience's awareness of itself as a participant. Artaud (1958), Grotowski (1968), and Stanislavski (1961) sought the instillation of emotion in the audience, to lead directly to a catharsis, following Aristotle's (1957) original notion that theater serves to purge terror and pity from the audience. Others, notably Brecht (1948), sought to distance the audience from the emotions of the play through the alienation effect.

> The epic theatre for Brecht was one where narrative had supremacy over drama, where the spectator became an

observer of the action, rather than a participant in the action, and was encouraged to face a certain situation and make decisions, rather than become involved in a situation and luxuriate in it...In epic theatre, reason played the primary role; feeling was secondary (Landy, 1986, p. 176)

Each of these approaches emphasizes a potentiality of audience experience.

The audience in the psychotherapy session does not consist of another person, but different psychic states of the therapist and the client. In fact, the therapist seeks to have the client psychically move from the point of view of the actor to that of the audience. On the one hand, the therapist is the witness and spectator of the patient's story, or drama, but in that the therapist has been cast as a character via the transference, he is an actor, too. The audience is created in psychotherapy by interpretation of the transference roles; that is, the therapist points out that what the client has been expressing in fact refers to another reality. A successful interpretation joins the observing egos of both participants, as the audience to the drama enacted by themselves in the transference. If the interpretation is premature, when the actors have not rounded, then the client's response will be a distant and intellectual one. If a degree of intensity has developed in the transference, and the client's internal character is fully present but not so strong as to possess him, then the interpretation will be followed by a powerful catharsis of emotion, for aesthetic distance has been achieved.

Catharsis

Scheff (1979), Landy (1983), and others have examined catharsis from the point of view of *aesthetic dis-*

tance. Aesthetic distance is that state of consciousness that is between, and balances, "distanced" intellectual observation of events and "under-distanced" emotional involvement in them. Catharsis of feeling occurs at the point of aesthetic distance when a stimulus is perceived as both real and not real. For example, a painting has aesthetic power if what is portrayed can be seen as real, but still as a painting. A Greek sculpture of a nude woman has aesthetic distance, pornography does not. If the audience thinks that the hero actually will be murdered on the stage, they do not achieve catharsis; they panic. They are not purged of terror, they are filled with it. On the other hand, if they view the drama with too great distance, the action leaves them cold and unemotional. Stanislavski points out that the actor must attain a state similar to this in that he must fully believe in the emotions of the character yet at the same time know that they are repeated experiences, not the actual ones (Moore, 1974). The actor, no matter how involved in his character, has to remember when to exit, to turn toward the audience, and project his voice.

> At aesthetic distance the individual plays roles of both participant and observer simultaneously, or he is able to move fluidly from one role to the other, as appropriate (Landy, 1983, p. 178)

Acting is the art of achieving this dual consciousness.

Likewise in psychotherapy, if the emotions are too strong and the client cannot distinguish transference from reality and actually views the therapist as sadistic or seductive, then catharsis is not achieved. If the client is not involved enough in the power of his unconscious emotions and feelings, not fully in role, then the insights attempted will not lead to catharsis. Catharsis occurs when there is a balance of emotion and observation, and an appreciation of the distinction between the reality of the therapy and the recalled traumas of the past relived in the therapy. "Aesthetic distance involves a balanced experience of a present and a past scene" (Scheff, 1979, p. 63). This is both a theatrical and a therapeutic moment. Catharsis, for audience or client, occurs with knowledge that the trauma is safely in the past, though the experience is recalled in the present. These moments are difficult to achieve and require many repeated opportunities to integrate fully into one's self. The process of "working through" involves the shifting back and forth between these modes of consciousness: first experience and then observation of the transferential roles reflecting the underlying "story" of the client's life.

> The transference thus forms a kind of intermediary realm between illness and real life, through which the journey from the one to the other must be made (Freud, 1914, p. 165)

The transference, he says, is like a playground. It is from these intermediary realms, these transitional, even transformational, playgrounds that the sources of creativity and healing spring. So many concepts attempt to capture this enigma: Winnicott's (1953) transitional object, which is and is not the self; Freud's (1914) sublimation, by which the impulse is and is not expressed; Rothenberg's (1987) homospatial and janusian processes, which rely on the coexistence of opposites; Langer's (1953) concepts of feeling and form, which need to be balanced; or Sartre's (1942) notion of becoming, that unique characteristic of the human being, "who is what he is not, and who is not what he is."

Each of these speaks to an elemental dialectic, still mysterious, shared by creative endeavors and the human spirit. It is in these arenas, these vague midlands between fantasy and reality that our selves are created, and our being resides.

Exiting

If we shadows have offended,
Think but this, and all is mended,
That you have but slumbered here,
While these visions did appear.
(Shakespeare, *A Midsummer Night's Dream*)

Thus, psychotherapy involves creating a stage, building characters, articulating a story, inviting an audience, and reaching catharsis. In this sense psychotherapy *strives* to be theater, a theater of the self, of the inner world; to be successful it needs to follow many of the same practices as good theater. A good therapy is in this sense consonant with a good play, only it is a play of one's own creating that had been previously veiled.

But what of the end? In theater the end inevitably comes, the curtain falls and the lights come up, and one goes home. In psychotherapy, can one ever close the curtain on the play of the inner world? While striving to be theater, psychotherapy ultimately aims to release us from theater. By making us aware of the play we have been compulsively reenacting, our internal characters are released, so they can return to their place in the *illud tempus* and allow us to go on with our lives. The range of personal exploration in therapy has been greater than real life, and yet one recognizes that it is less than real life, as one awakens to the present and to new possibilities of being. This is both a relief and a loss, for few things match the intensity of our inner lives.

As we walk down the stairs of the theater, or our therapist's office, put on our coats and walk onto the street, taking a deep breath, we say to ourselves, "Yes, what went on in there I recognize; and I will carry it with me forever, as a memory. It is part of who I am, but I am released from it." This is the play. This is Fate. This is the given. It happened. Now I can continue.

What greater gift can there be than that?

3

Ego Rhythm in Art and Therapy

In describing "ego rhythm" as the oscillation back and forth between a fragmented formless state and an organized, logical perceptual gestalt, Ehrenzweig (1967) amplifies what I consider to be a core aspect of the true self. This center of energy provides the foundation for a self that constantly attempts to organize impressions and experience into some type of cohesive unity. Described in slightly different terms, one can view this flow of energy as an ongoing movement between primary and secondary processes, the former being characterized by unbound energy, timelessness, and shifting perceptions and the latter by linear definition and organization. The self, then, is constantly undergoing modification as energy is organized and reorganized from the inside out and vice versa. If kept

95

alive, ego rhythm is an aspect of our selfhood that gives each of our "selves" a means by which to continually grow and be reborn. As we move deeply into the center of the self where energy is unbound and free-formed and then back out, we make new symbolic connections and self-definitions. For some individuals, this rhythm holds little meaning, while still others have lost their ability to listen to these deep internal messages. It is, therefore, the rediscovery of this rhythm that I see as one of the essentials of therapeutic treatment as well as a critical part of the treatment process itself.

Connecting ego rhythm to the therapeutic process demands the therapist's attunement to the intrapsychic rhythm of the patient. The therapist must then be able to tap his or her own rhythm to create an interpersonal rhythm, if you will, in the transitional space created between them. This transitional space between patient and therapist is reminiscent of the transitional space between infant and mother that is described by Winnicott (1953) as an intermediate area that lies neither inside nor outside the members of the dyad, but somewhere in between, bridging subjective and objective realities. It is a space where two minds join yet remain separate, creating a dual level of consciousness. In tapping his or her own ego rhythm, the therapist moves back and forth between dwelling in the unstructured myriad of senses and feelings deep within that are formed in response to the patient, and then moving outward to give shape and structure to these impressions in symbols and images which he or she then utilizes in the service of connecting the patient to his or her own ego rhythm. It is my contention that until the patient can touch his or her formless state, he/she has not really reached the nexus for reconstructive change.

As treatment evolves, the energy constellations shift and the images and symbols utilized by the therapist are reorganized to parallel the shifts in transference and countertransference. Needless to say, the ever-changing flow of vibrations of psychic forces, such as love, hate, and sexuality, require a variety of interpretive frames on the part of the therapist. Experiencing and responding appropriately to these forces coming from the centers of our patients requires a delicate reading of nuances on the part of the therapist. The organization and reorganization of the transitional space becomes the heart of analytic work.

My own sense of this rhythm has evolved as I've struggled to forge an integration between a psychology of the artist and psychoanalytic theory/technique. This has been a very personal challenge for me stemming from a need to make whole the intuitive–sensual–artistic and cognitive–analytic parts of myself that came from the female and male sides of my family, respectively. The sculpture studio became an arena where I rediscovered a piece of myself, a piece that has since become central in how I work as an artist, as a therapist with my patients, and in viewing analysis. As a sculptor, I've discovered that when I try to control the material I'm working with, I become disconnected from my work and create a mess. I've learned that each sculpture, each material, has a rhythm of its own, which, if entered into and joined, gives clues for direction that can then be utilized when I step out of this "oneness" to give form to the material. There is a movement back and forth between being part of the material and then separate; or, put another way, an oscillation between formlessness and form, which defines the rhythm of the creative experience. In working with stone, the subtle indentations and crevices in the material itself suggest directions in which to move. Likewise, in working with patients, opposing an individual's natural internal rhythm, or attempting to impose your own rhythm, may well increase resistance. Avoiding a collision with a patient's core defense usually makes very good therapeutic sense.

Upon viewing my own work, I see a repetitive image that becomes a metaphor of sorts for ego rhythm and my use of it in therapy as well as in my art. My stonework often has a hole or holes in it that feel quite familiar to me, as they reflect a long-standing piece of who I am. Part of me looks for the rhythm in the stone, in the piece; but deep inside, there is also a place that I see as separate and alone. I call it the schizoid part of myself. At one time this schizoid part functioned as a place where I could escape and withdraw from the world. Now I view that schizoid part of me as a receptacle for particles of experience, where all the partial images, vague sensory impressions, half-recognized thoughts, and subtle sensations can congeal and take form. These holes and what they represent in terms of the movement back and forth between a more formless state of fleeting impressions and energy flow and a more cognitive state of organizing and giving form create the link, for me, between the creative and therapeutic processes. In both instances, this oscillation allows me to connect with a deep form of nonverbal communication and to access a valuable source for direction.

While my appreciation of ego rhythm came from my own work as an artist, most of us have experienced the oscillation I'm referring to as ego rhythm. It's the oscillation we feel at a concert when we're swept away by the music and become one with it, then step back to observe it, moving in and out of the experience, or when we read literature and alternately become part of the story and then the observer of the action. Creative individuals who utilize intuition or fantasy are familiar with this rhythm as they create the space for themselves to wait for particles of experience to congeal into a sense or understanding that points the way for therapeutic direction.

I'd like to describe a treatment case in order to demonstrate some of these issues. I recall it was 1958 and I was starting out as a therapist in a local mental health clinic. I had been discharged from the army and had worked for a few years in another agency. My analytic training had started and I was very excited about beginning to work intensively with this case. I well recall my first meeting with this woman. My office was on a second floor, and I happened to look out the window to catch a glimpse of my patient as she drove up to my office. She was driving a red convertible with the top down, music blaring from the car. An attractive, well-built blonde in a tightly fitting sweater stepped from the car, slammed the door, and started for the office with a self-assured stride. Her perfume filled the room and she flashed me a radiant smile. I could almost hear drumbeats in the background. Without saying a word out loud, she shouted "notice me, I mean business." Libidinal tension was high. There was no question about my immediate sense of intrigue and involvement in this case!

As she began to speak in hushed tones, an image of the movie, "The Postman Always Rings Twice," ran through my mind, which scared me. I had the fantasy that somehow I was being set up, or was being asked to join my patient as a partner in crime. Having no idea where all this would lead, I listened to her story. Her husband, a policeman, would come home at nights drunk and would beat her up. She wanted out of the marriage, but she didn't know how to leave him. She was afraid that if she made any move to leave, he would kill her. Now, as I started to get a sense of what her history was, I began to notice that every time I attempted to move in and ask a question, the image would come to mind of a cat going across my face and scratching me. I'd ask her, "What did that mean?" "Could you tell me something more," and invariably, what I'd feel in her response was something that came across as, "Stupid, why are you asking that question?" With every intervention, she would glare at me. As my fleeting images coalesced, I realized that the erotic atmosphere had disappeared, and with it the provocative vamp. In its place was a wild, terror-stricken alley cat. Perhaps it had been the glare in her eyes, the wild look, the body tension, or the feeling that she would scratch my eyes out if I moved in too fast in trying to make contact with her. One thing was clear, and that was the need to approach slowly; when you're in a room with an alley cat, you move in very carefully, because if you don't, out will come the claws and she will hiss. Scattered impressions, then, that were both picked up from my patient on a sensory level and from somewhere deep inside myself had oscillated back and forth in my mind until they had congealed into images that were utilized in treatment.

Both the images of the alley cat and the accomplice

in crime were important in our analytic work throughout the first year. I worked very slowly and paid a lot of
attention to the center of wildness, the primitive energy, in this woman. I spoke in hushed tones, rarely
attempted interpretive connections, remained mildly
questioning, and offered plenty of space for reflection.
This addressed both the frightened, wild alley cat and
the boss woman who called the shots and directed the
action. It was almost as though I meditated on her wildness, feeling every move until I could feel her pulse. A
dance emerged between us that slowly calmed the alley
cat and allowed her to feel me as nonthreatening. It was
as though she started to purr. In this year when there
were no interpretations and few reflections, her life improved immensely. She left her husband and life was
much better.

A new phase in treatment began to unfold as subtly and slowly my images of my patient as a rough-and-
tumble alley cat evolved into a stray cat who was
hungry and looking to be fed. Part of the change in
emotional tone had to do with her becoming more demanding and angry if I maintained my previously
hushed stance. Her face was now, at times, taut and
sad. At the same time, I'd find myself thinking about
"Pygmalion." I saw the street ragamuffin look toward
me to be wise and thoughtful; someone to educate her
about life. You work with a street ragamuffin in a very
different way from an alley cat; the rhythm is quite different. I became more helpful and supportive as she'd
bring in problems she was having with her children. All
the time we worked this way, I worked on the assumption that her children were a vehicle for her looking at
the lost "me" that floated between us in treatment. She

would talk about her children's problems with reading, not attending school, other kids picking on them, and so forth. I was careful not to be too directive and wouldn't give her the answers, but we would explore these problems in some detail. Along the way, she'd start to cry. Now every time she'd hit some critical point and cry more than she could handle, she'd go to a bar and pick up a man. That would be the end of the tears for a while, until with a little more courage, she'd cry a bit more. This all remained within the context of talking about the children. Unlike our first phase, I started to offer more empathic reflections and be more available as a deep loneliness filtered into our relationship and my patient struggled to find something to cover her deep black hole of pain and despair. The emphasis was very much on the self and the bottomless black sense of formlessness that pervaded the transference–countertransference relationship. She did seem to hear my interpretive efforts. It was during this phase that she started to construct a narrative structure of her life.

We began to explore her family. She came from a background that was quite deprived. Her mother was extremely depressed and very unavailable, while her father seemed to have been a very strange man who was erotically attached to his daughter. He'd ask his daughter to put make-up on him and they'd lie in bed together. There was a good deal of fondling that went on, though for the most part the patient felt frozen. In late adolescence, the daughter was able to extricate herself from this relationship through her connection to her peers, and she developed a tough veneer and sexually provocative stance that seemed to help her and gave her the sense of being much older than she appeared. She recalled these experiences with a sense of paralysis, and I understood much better both why she had been paralyzed during our first phase of treatment and why it took her so long to invite me into her kitchen, so to speak, to allow me to feed and educate her.

This went on for another year as she oscillated back and forth between her states of depression and her attempts to find safety in picking up local men. Her children's lives stabilized as they began to do well in school and develop friends. Then something again shifted in our relationship and a new atmosphere entered the relationship as I found myself humming the German war song "Madeleine," a song referring to a Nazi soldier singing about the girl he left behind. Images of Marlene Dietrich filled my mind. I must have come quite close to where my patient was at that moment in treatment, because as I was humming this song to myself, she said to me, "Look, Robbins, we've been seeing one another long enough, when are we going to get down to business?" I had been seeing her for a long time, and she wondered if my interest in her were more than just professional. The erotic transference was in full bloom, and the sexual interest that she was exhibiting now was quite different from that of our first meeting. At first, her eroticism had been simply a manifestation of anxiety, I think, and a need for creature-comfort contact. Now, she heard me and she reflected upon my interpretations. A narrative sense of her history slowly emerged in terms of the problems with her father. She began to see connections between how she saw me, her wishes and fears of sexual contact, and the reasons that men were both powerful and frightening at the same time. Our relationship had moved from a narcissistic one to an object-oriented give-and-take exchange. I found the German girlfriend accessible. She asked for contact and welcomed help in organizing her life story. As she deepened her understanding, the transient relationships with men subsided. During the course of these two phases of treatment, the loose, wild energy that had been so prevalent in the first phase had now become a core, a sense of center, a place to touch and use to help integrate pieces of experience into new integrations of the self.

What had evolved was the beginning of a bridge between the narrative of her life and the primitive inner core of wildness, of energy. There was now a flow, a rhythm, an oscillation between the center with its shifting impressions, images, and affects and a secondary level of processing that was constantly attempting to organize impressions to make sense out of experience.

Arnheim (1982) describes two elements of composition that offer another description of this process. He calls one element of composition the pull toward the center. The other element is called the Cartesian grid. In terms of the pull toward the center, if you look at any artwork, there is always some central focus where your eye is drawn. There is also, however, in any good work of art, energy that goes from the picture outward. In treatment, the patient's capacity to move deeply into the center of the self, where energy becomes unbound, ultimately provides the source for the emergence of new symbolic connections. The thematic grid, on the other hand, provides an internal structure that channels the flow of energy from the inside to the outside. In the best of therapeutic and creative sessions, the analyst, like the artist creating a balanced composition in a painting, facilitates this shifting and merging of primary and secondary modes of communication where there is a constant reordering of new forms and connections. The interplay of these two vital forces of inside and outside and the integration of these forces, which are characterized by a narrative sense of one's personal history and inner core of vital energy, become the aesthetic frame of treatment. Some patients enter treatment without a vital center, others with an enormous grid of history that doesn't quite connect to the internal energy, and some, like this patient, with an intensity of vibrant energy but without the balance of a structure to contain and organize the self. Here, treatment process became a frame to balance the anchor of a narrative structure and the rich source of growth and change alive in this patient's vital core. What went on, then, became a dialectic between self and object in the transitional space between patient and therapist.

I'd like to return briefly to a part of this woman's treatment in which we focused on the depressive–schizoid part of herself as she went through her black, depressive phase. The process offers both an example of one patient's ego rhythm and the therapeutic work with it, a point frequently reached in the course of analytic treatment. This patient's way of dealing with blackness was to feel the blackness and the sadness for a while, and then bounce away from it. She would break out of her "deadness" by picking up men in bars and plunge into exciting, chaotic affairs that would mobilize the life around her and temporarily distract her from her depression. Insisting that she remain with the blackness and depression would only have served to violate her own particular rhythm of healing. She required freedom to find her own way in treatment in her own time. For a while I even took the position of enjoying the acting out while at the same time gently reminding her of what she was running from. My goal was to help her respect and care for her character defenses rather than to see them as the enemy. All too often, therapists forget that these defenses have been extremely important survival mechanisms. For our patients, however, there often arises feeling of shame regarding their defenses, rather than appreciating their importance. Our job then as therapists is to help patients accept, if not love, their resistance to change. By so doing, the paradox of treatment becomes self-evident: Resistance becomes a bridge for movement and change. Now the patient experiences self-acceptance rather than a wish to punish himself through therapeutic inertia. In this case, as we worked back and forth between touching the sadness and running from it and doing interpretive work while giving definition to the depression's own characteristic shading, weight, depth, and substance, the heaviness of my patient's life gradually became less devastating and pervasive. The transitional space gave her the room to move between oneness and separateness and offered her renewed strength to reexperience the empty black-gray formless state of her childhood.

In summary, I want to reiterate a basic premise of treatment: To help patients rediscover and respect their own natural rhythms of change. In this hurried and pressured age of ours, accomplishing this goal becomes a particularly formidable task, especially when compounded by our patients' identification with introjected processes that by their very nature are disrhythmic. In my own caseload, I constantly am faced with patients who have lost their own rhythm, others who can't hear their own internal drumbeat, and others who have lost their ability to hear both the intuitive parts of themselves and those parts that organize their reflections in vibrant, exciting forms of affirmative decorations of existence. All of us from time to time may lose our internal rhythm. Yet, as analysts we have an obligation to ourselves as well as to our patients to rediscover this lost oscillation from the inside to the outside so that energy and form become intrinsic parts of an ongoing identity formation. This rhythm, I believe, is central and basic to the very nature of the treatment process and demands attention and nourishment. In the next chapter, I will describe how the atunement to ego rhythms becomes a prime requisite for the development of therapeutic empathy.

4

A Psychoaesthetic Approach to Empathic Contact

As a fledgling therapist, I functioned with the naive notion that therapeutic empathy was relatively simple and straightforward. Reflecting a patient's feelings, I thought, demanded only a modicum of sensitivity and objectivity. Now, after years of experiencing the complexities and nuances of empathic relatedness, I am aware of the enormous demands of personal artistry in the delivery of such a response. The mixture of verbal and nonverbal attunement can range from a simple raised eyebrow accompanied by a mild question to a rather complicated affective, cognitive, and perceptual response to a patient. The shades of meaning conveyed by verbal intonations and use of personal images and the level of intimacy in the exchange all add up to this therapeutic statement: "I understand; I am with you."

The empathic response can be penetrating, for on occasion the therapist must mirror back a deep unconscious reflection of the patient. By contrast, a very surface mirroring response may be all that is needed to communicate to the patient that you are empathically connected to the flow of material. Thus, when and how a therapist imparts empathy becomes an aesthetic act that will call upon a variety of different levels of consciousness.

In a recent volume expressly devoted to the subject of empathy (Lichtenberg, Bornstein, and Silver, 1984), one of the contributors, Pinchas Noye, attributes three basic components to empathy:

1. A special sensitivity to understand other persons accurately
2. A particular perceptual mode
3. A tendency to project one's personality (self) into the personality (self) of the other

He further elaborates that sensitivity is determined by primary process, whereas the other two components are determined by secondary-process formations. These three components at their most mature level are so integrated that they cannot be differentiated from one another. In pathological development, on the other hand, discrepancies can occur both in terms of one component's relative dominance over another and in differing developmental levels.

This line of thinking seems to parallel some of the basic research and material advanced by Daniel Stern (1985). He, however, breaks empathy down into four distinct sequential processes:

1. The resonance of feeling state
2. The abstraction of empathic knowledge from experience of emotional resonance
3. The integration of abstracted empathic knowledge into empathic response
4. A transient role identification

We can infer from this perspective that Stern postulates emotional resonance between mother and child as a base for the development of a sensitive interpersonal awareness. Noye (Lichtenberg *et al.*, 1984) believes that this process cannot easily be altered by therapy, but his "perceptual mode" appears very similar to Stern's processes 2 and 3. In reference to Stern's fourth component, a variety of countertransference issues relating to the professional self of the therapist may well contribute to her skill in developing transient role identification. These latter processes appear to be open for modification either through therapy supervision or training groups. Within these areas, the individual's fluidity of boundary formation, flexibility or rigidity of character structure, and capacity for a dual level of consciousness all appear to be basic ingredients that can be modified through intensive training experience.

In addition to the above-mentioned attributes of empathy, the therapist's capacity to communicate a wide variety of modes of relatedness may further contribute to his skill in empathic contact. More specifically, we refer to a therapist's skill in the sensitive employment of metaphors that have either a visual, auditory, or kinesthetic origin and that, in turn, can match the patient's unique use of language. Along the same lines, the therapist's sensitivity to the patient's gestures and way of moving also contribute to skill in empathic relatedness. Finally, how a therapist utilizes images to organize her sensations may make a further contribution in understanding and utilizing empathic contact. Although implied in the above paragraphs, we want to emphasize that the ability to integrate complex levels of seeing, feeling, and knowing are part of this complex responsiveness to patients. In short, empathic relatedness implies a synthesis of nonverbal and verbal communication and is determined by the therapist's capacity to synthesize and organize and respond to multiple levels of communication. This capacity will be based on the therapist's integration and organization of drives, object relations, and structural integration.

This being the case, therapists must learn to speak the language of their patients. For example, hearing a patient who is goal-oriented and organized in his manner of speaking demands a different form of empathic matching than does the patient who is poetic and metaphorical. Seeing, then, empathic contact as a creative and imaginative therapeutic act, we must call forth different levels of our own internal object lives to either match or contrast a patient's style of communication. These may range from being soothing to feisty in a cognitively articulate way. This creative act is one that calls upon the conscious and unconscious processes of both therapeutic parties and exists within a unique "therapeutic space."

Finally, empathic relatedness cannot be separated from countertransference problems. Emotional issues that stem from therapists' past histories as well as typical inductions create continual pressures that interfere with the maintenance of empathic responsiveness. In the following vignette, a mature therapist presents a case in a countertransference group where empathic relatedness to his patient becomes the chief focus of discussion. No attempt will be made to describe this presentation in depth. The focus will be on the fragments that bear special relevance to empathic issues. The presenter, Jim, had discussed this case in a previous session, but left the group feeling dissatisfied with his understanding of the material. One week later, Jim returned to the group and explored the case in greater depth. The patient, experienced by the therapist as a whiny, complaining child, requests succor and at the same time provokes sadism. While the therapist insulates himself from the perpetually irritating side of the patient, he complains of impotence in making contact with her. For Jim, this whole developmental area of experience, namely, the whiny, out-of-sorts 2-year-old, seemed to be completely dissociated from his initial attempt to discuss the case. I assumed that in Jim's independent, take-charge stance, a whiny, demanding child was not a very acceptable image or experience likely to receive a sympathetic response in terms of his own internal representations. Jim's psychotherapy style was basically confrontive and direct. The softer, more soothing aspects of his presentation with patients was not always available. I think it would be fair to say that the father inside of Jim was far more available and touchable than the mother, the latter being a source of weakness and coldness. If anything, the soft, resonant tones in Jim seemed to be assimilated from the father. This case, however, presented its own particular wrinkle. The child behind the whine is struggling to hold on to some very basic survival mechanisms. She is fright-

ened of loss of contact and equally scared of being sexually assaulted by an eroticized mother and father. This
eroticization is communicated by both parents on a
very subtle and dissociated level. In response to the
patient's induction, the group proceeded to discuss
firmness and softness and recommended that the therapist avoid the tough male edge that the patient unconsciously provokes by her whining. Thus, emotional
resonance with the patient's manifest affect becomes
then a complex issue. We obviously do not always mirror what our patient sets forth in this kind of situation.
We are firm, quiet, sometimes irritated, but very clear
and cognitive. This becomes a centering experience for
the patient, since she has divorced a cognitive understanding from an underlying fear and impulse.

As a therapist, Jim felt uncomfortable calling on
the female side of himself. He mocked this role, and in
response to the group's recommendation for soft, female resonance, responded, "I'll just have to put on my
tutu." It came all too close to some of his own pregenital issues. The group, in turn, responded with soft,
supportive tones, and often with good-natured laughter, offering a nonthreatening model of Mr. Rogers for
Jim to follow in his treatment. In this suggestion was a
soft acknowledgment of Jim's dilemma. Finding the appropriate image to facilitate resonance then became an
extremely important part of tuning up therapeutic empathic relatedness. We saw how the group became a
model for communicating softness and at the same time
creating a channel to make it possible for Jim to communicate this affect to his patient.

Thus, through the prototype of the figure of Mr.
Rogers, Jim arrived at an image that provided a conduit

for empathic contact. Empathy and understanding then in a climate that is supportive and nonintrusive and which offers clarity and specificity help to further the patient's self-definition. The need for physical comfort and control by the infant patient was dramatically acted out in the group. Jim played out the irritable 2-year-old while the mothers responded and attempted to soothe their therapist's "child." Through this small, dramatic role-playing, Jim kinesthetically experienced the world of the 2-year-old, a prime requisite for making empathic contact with this patient. Feeling her fear of sexual assault was far more difficult as this was very buried behind the character structure. On the surface, the patient was full of rigid morality that served as her anchor and connection to mother. Jim needed also to experience the polar opposite of rigid sexual morality so that he could feel both the patient and her connection to the mother. Finally the group helped Jim with his need to insulate himself from the patient as a defense against some of his own irritation that the patient unconsciously provokes.

The object then of aesthetically working with the countertransference is neither to deny nor to dissociate from the provocation, but to offer a container for the reactive sadism while responding to the lost child who knows no other way to gain attention than to be a whiner. Expressing some of the irritation may not interfere with being empathically connected, for this patient knows all too well what her effect is on others. Offering a cognitive understanding of the motivations and developmental problems of the whiny child, however, can offer a structure to the patient's inner world.

A few highlights of this presentation require further elaboration.

1. Feeling one's way into the transitional space of patient and therapist involves a concentrated attention to the bodily projections of both therapeutic participants. The images accruing out of this experience become the play area within which to conduct interpretive work. In a rather simplistic fashion, the therapist can apprehend maternal or paternal imagos that respond to a particular infantile projection from the patient. It is rare that the therapeutic material is so clear-cut. In the case under discussion, there is a mixture of preoedipal and oedipal components playing into one another. The therapist, hearing both a frightened, lost girl who whines and provokes in order to make contact, but who is equally frightened of soothing contact, must offer a supportive but clear and concise parental response that maintains a semblance of male directness while remaining basically nonintrusive. The Mr. Rogers image seemed to be a perfect receptacle for a 2-year-old who has no idea why she is crying, but who indeed needs support. The soft, clear, and slow cadence that surrounds Mr. Rogers' image became a psychic organizer to move into the patient's psychic space. Here, the image provided the therapist a means to both feel the patient's psychic use of space and at the same time provide some way of kinesthetically finding a road map that will provide a means of pacing interventions and contacts with the patient's internal representations. It is important to note, however, that in real life, it is a most unusual parent or therapist who can live up to the image of Mr. Rogers. As parents, as well as therapists, we may well be irritated, exasperated, and out of sorts with our children or patients. I do not feel that the expression of these affects will necessarily interfere or

runs contrary to these affects and the occasional expression of them may help facilitate that quiet centeredness that is so important for the crying, provocative 2-year-old.

2. The imagos that are generated from this transitional space are fluid and move as both patient and therapist enter different phases of treatment. Once again, the interpretive style changes according to the nature of the nonverbal context. Please refer to the elaboration of this process in Chapter 3. We must remember that these images are often primary-process oriented and require a cognitive framework so that there can be a sensitive employment of them in patient–therapist relatedness.

3. When a patient's sadomasochistic defense is utilized to cope with object loss, enormous countertransference issues are stimulated. The 2-year-old's insistence on complete control of the object becomes a regressive magnet toward fusion. In treatment, as in child-rearing, the maternal object can feel angry, controlled, frustrated, or oversolicitous. Jim's countertransference response was to take a somewhat detached position in this process. Another therapist might overidentify, become angry, or be subtly seductive as a means of coping with this anxiety. The transference–countertransference issue becomes even more complex as the patient's inexplicable crying disguises rage as well as a fear of closeness in spite of her wish for soothing. Again, the image of Mr. Rogers comes to mind as a solution embodying a presence that is stable, constant, nonintrusive, and supportive. We must emphasize once again, however, that this quiet centeredness cannot be phony or inauthentic. Centeredness can

emerge from many different emotional sources and therapeutic personalities, and it is important to realize that even the best of us will get knocked off our centeredness at times and not be completely present with our patients. The creative image that facilitates a patient–therapist relatedness arises out of the mix of both the internal worlds of therapist and patient.

In summary, the reexperiencing of an emotional resonance of the mother with a petulant 2-year-old becomes an important developmental reawakening for Jim. Playing a whole variety of roles in a supervisory session becomes an important learning experience to broaden the therapist's capacity for transient role-playing and patient trial identification. Providing an experiential context for the exploration of mother and child in the 2-year-old period, then, creates enough cognitive understanding to be easily translated to the case material.

Let us now review some of the dimensions of empathic relatedness that interfere with the various layers of personality organization that filter through this case presentation. From a defensive ego point of view, we did not avoid some of our irritation with the patient's masochistic defenses, but combined annoyance and frustration with a clear, concise understanding of what the patient was avoiding. Then, we regained our "Mr. Rogers stance" and maintained a quiet, centered presence. Ultimately, we attempted to expand the patient's verbal self to allow sexual energy to enter into an emerging new identity. We also attempted to play with the patient's rigid introject of the mother and helped provide an empathic contact with the patient's inner self that needed room and distance from this oppression.

The variety in these levels required humor, firmness, authenticity, and creativeness—a very tall order for a most complex patient. But then again, we only have to be "good enough" therapists, not perfect.

5

Moving into the Black Spot

Arthur Robbins and Priscilla Rodgers

As both patient and therapist experience the deep, oscillating movement of form and formlessness, the primitive layers of self-organization emerge. Blackness, emptiness, and gray numbness slowly enter into the therapeutic matrix. This chapter will explore a particular aspect of the psychoaesthetic experience; namely, moving into the black spot.

All too often therapists view the "blackness" of pain, depression, despair, and helplessness as monodimensional and the diagnostic categories of "schizoid" and "depressive" as tightly bounded and separate. I would like to suggest that it is not enough to talk about depression in either/or terms; as either indicating aggression directed toward the self or a state of hopelessness, helplessness, and low self-esteem. These are flat categorical descriptions that do not really do justice to the complex, multifaceted state of emotional blackness that exists to some extent in all of us. What I see in my clinical practice is a dynamic continuum from depressive to schizoid, with blackness moving into states of death, despair, and helplessness, as well as a black, empty void or a clinging grayness. In its more positive dimensions, black becomes an ethereal poetic, a directed power, a spiritual connectiveness, or a sensual black velvety elegance. In its more pathological form, our "black spot" can either be covered over by a "false self" structure, restricting an organic integration of affects, or it can invade every orifice of our being, like a heavy dark cloud, lying fallow, creating the paradox of still energy being experienced as diffuse, unbound, and inarticulated. In either instance, the boundary issues of self and other have never been fully defined, for our very black diffuseness has not developed toward a state of transformation, and the dynamic process of loss, death, rage, and regeneration becomes truncated by an overpowering sense of pain. The psychic awareness of inner and outer realities blurs and dims; rage at the other remains a muted faint echo. In this unending black pit, there is no forgiveness, indeed gray-blackness never transforms itself into a force that is fueled by a destructive wish to kill the object. In the "false self" position, the pain and rage become displaced; yet, the repetition of living out separation and loss creates an endless parade of happenstance, for the self never makes peace with the slippery ghosts that become all too fused with concrete reality.

Drawing upon my sensibilities and language as an artist, I think of "blackness" as having many shades of meaning, many textures, many forms, and demanding a constant awareness of such elements as balance, volume, space, and shading, all of which have their psychic parallels. For instance, balance relates to a subtle awareness of the polarities of affects, volume speaks of the heaviness or lightness in the transitional space, while shading deals with the subtle tactile nuances of communications that convert raw affect into luminosity. These elements coalesce in particular images and connections and are all clearly translatable into the metaphor of the interplay between black and white. The integration of these elements into an aesthetic whole takes form on a variety of different levels.

The artist offers the viewer an aesthetic affective matrix of these elements in dynamic motion. Ad Reinhardt (Rose, 1953), noted for his studies in blackness, offers one of the most striking verbal appreciations of the richness of black through poetic reflections entitled "Black."

> *Black is negation.*
> Ministers, priests, *solemn token of absolute principles*
> *Sure, inexorable*
> Erudite philosophy, homely aphorism, proverbs, adages
> *Infinite, inevitable*
> Complete insoluble mystery
> Funeral
> (Dislike of black, clinging to life, naivete)
> (Superstitions, fear)
> *Unconditional demands*
>
> Black, morbidity, despair?   Blue, carnal man regenerated,

made
spiritual
Death
Inevitability of fate
Nothingness, negation

Worldly, immutable, stark worldly-wise
Regal (not pompous)   universal, sober
Dignified (not officious)   patience, perseverance

True substance, weight

Sophisticated
Passivity   Deliberation, introspection
Non-exciting
Arbitrary, if not artificial

Private life different than public life
Schizophrenic
Mystery
Not carefree
Game, wit, cleverness, removed from the ordinary

Conventionality
Leave real personalities at home
              evening clothes
Assume a proper, polite manner
Mother-pastel, Father-darker shades
Concentration on self.

The implications here are important, for if there are indeed many dimensions in which the affect of blackness
exists and can be explored, then it behooves us as thera-

pists to be sensitive to the number of resonant holding environments that may be generated in response to black as an ego state.

I'd like to share a dialogue with you, between artist therapist Priscilla Rodgers and myself, in which she discusses her paintings and I respond to her art form as though it were a therapeutic communication. First she will reflect upon her creative process and paintings in a general way, and I will offer counterpoint with psychological commentary as a way to present the intimate relationship between aesthetic and psychological dynamics. Then she will proceed to explore her painting, entitled "The Black Garden," and through this intimate dialogue, the reader can participate in the transformational values and possibilities of living and moving through a state of blackness. The following dialogue projects a rich account of the very focus of blackness a patient may also present and gives an account of the processing that takes place in working through a state of blackness. Priscilla begins:

My work is built up as a field of shifting lines and tones, a world of possible boundaries in the making.

> Priscilla's transitional space provides an open and fluid field of energy. As a therapist, I want to make contact with her center and experience the various levels of energy that radiate out in the session. My approach will be equally flowing and open.

I am drawn toward nonrepresentational forms where I can float between the freedom of the unbounded and the necessity of definition. Fragments of recognizable objects and organic forms enter in and become part of the dynamic.

In therapy, the holding environment would be both
loose, clear, open, yet defined, paralleling the inner energy that Priscilla interjects in our relationship.
  Though I would be laid-back, I sense that she can
appreciate a warm, but not confining approach to her
communications.

As I reflect, it seems that the process of painting
serves to punctuate my stream of awareness. Often I
have composed paintings like music, imagining a
sound quality corresponding to the visual elements.
Music is in some way closer to the kind of primal tone
which sources my work, seeming less devoted to the
representational.

Priscilla's communications are composed of musical
rhythms and tones that move very near the early core of
affective state of mother and child. The child and
mother make very early contact regarding pain, discomfort, and pleasure. Listening to Priscilla's voice,
with all its intonations and subtle tones, may be an important key in understanding a very core issue of
mother and child.

I begin my work with no plan, and no particular
external object from which to work. Instead, I work
from a build-up of sensations, images, colors, and feelings from within that are spontaneously brought together through an inner ordering principle which
remains mysterious.

Once again I am reminded that Priscilla needs plenty of
space to find her own particular rhythm with its unique
inflections and direction.

I look at the blank canvas and ask for something to
show itself from within. I begin, often, with a few faint
lines—mainly directional movements, the barest shap-

ings of space. As the process evolves, subtle images, edges, and visual occasions will stir me, and I begin to work, choosing what I will amplify and what direction the picture will take. I never know what the work will become, and that is what both attracts me to the activity and also creates the enormous anxiety of never being sure whether I will be capable of resolving and working it through, or whether I will be able to accept it as having come from my activity upon possibility.

> I suspect that Priscilla may suddenly create anxiety situations in order for her to go through the process of mastery. Will this be an important aspect of her own internal rhythm?

I work back and forth between fusion and delineation, creating lines that dance over the surface, forming partial boundaries—lines that go just far enough to keep the picture together but not so far that the picture becomes static. The rhythm must remain on the edge of chaos and yet bring about a harmony and equilibrium that looks as though it might shift again at any moment. The design is integrated so that there is trust that the shift will produce another design. They are pictures on the edge of falling apart, built of nothing but strokes of color and "accidental" form. In depending on the spontaneous and perhaps accidental, I am reaching toward an instinctual level, and level of self whereby images arise that are not rationally planned.

> I become even more sure of my initial suspicion: Does Priscilla create situations where she comes near the edge of falling apart as a means of mastering some very early developmental problem? Will some of these deep swings be ultimately introduced in our relationship?

In particular, I note that the descent into the unbounded layer of my psyche, or my primary process, wherein I face the unknown white of my canvas without a plan and begin to create out of chaos, is like a death. The creative process, then, becomes one of death and return to form, to material meaning. The process of delving into the unbounded and creating form from what issues from that experience brings me close to a relationship with mortality. I realized, on reflecting on my artistic past in preparation for this discussion of my work, that I really found my voice, as I call it, in art—really began to understand what I wanted to do through art and what excited me about it—shortly after my father was diagnosed with terminal cancer. My mother had always been a sickly woman, though often vibrant in style, and had come close to death several years earlier. My work became a way of mastering death, of coming to know it, or, as the Buddhists say, of practicing it.

> Priscilla's blackness and schizoid void may be an important pivotal place to rediscover a more central feeling of self. Will she bring these moods of utter despair and death into the transference relationship? Involved, then, will be issues of dependence and fears that no one will be there to hold her.

Also, both of my parents, though capable of a great deal of liveliness in behavior, were depressive in character and subject to periods of great unreachability. It is so normal for me to assume this distance that it was difficult for me to see this as pivotal in my choice of work. That I do not work from objects in the outside world may point to this distance that I naturally take from it. I have always looked within for resources that I could not ever be sure of finding in the external world.

Hence, I searched for a reservoir of aliveness within that I could depend on. I think that the anxiety that comes up for me when I do not paint comes from the fact that I have not checked in with this world for some time and become anxious that it may have deserted me. Left to deal emotionally with myself early on, I had to contain quite a bit of inner chaos that was not bounded, and I practice in my artwork to order this, with the help of my trust in a "hidden order of art" and of self.

> With all her openness and accessibility, I suspect that she may well take charge of the treatment and become very independent and autonomous, and we may fail to contact that infantile screaming self beneath the "autonomy."

That I will often cut things up and reposition them in a new way is perhaps another way of trying to master feelings of fragmentation in the family. I spent much of my family life trying to rescue the community unit (unconsciously of course), and I am struck again by the way the compositions are held together with an on-edge rhythm. A falling form will be rescued by a line placed just so to catch it, and this rhythm will flutter across the canvases.

> At a certain point in treatment my laid-back and gentle rhythm may change as Priscilla introduces material that requires a tying up of past and present. Herein lies some of the key to treatment. Can she depend enough on me to trust some of these interpretive interventions?

Especially in some of my drawings that begin with a felt sense of a mythical theme, or one that evolves into more organic feeling forms, the images are hinted at, never fully formed, never brought out completely. It is more important that they can remain fluid, can change if they wish. As well as illuminating a philosophy of change and a mirror of the creative process itself, on a more personal note, I think this carefully mirrors a strong defense of my own and my family's—that something must always remain hidden. What directly affects us or moves us is never talked about, never revealed. Nor can we approach the sacred experience. It is kept slightly shrouded, though implied. Often in my paintings there are intimations of a source of light coming from behind, as if the fleeting images on the surface were obstructing my view of something real behind. These issues are, of course, not limited to personal familial experience, but are existential. Yet, the purely personalistic dynamics are available as metaphor as are wider interpretations.

> I hear Priscilla's half-formed subtle intonations and senses. I must pay special attention to facilitate further definition and clarity to her communications, for she has relied all too much on a very secret private self.

"The Black Garden"

This painting was done very shortly after my mother's death (Fig. 6). It is part of a group of paintings and drawings called "The Black Garden." Most of my paintings up until this time had been very colorful, but still, I am told, had the pull and intensity of the black which pervades this one. Working improvisationally, I began here with a black field, allowing the piece to dialogue with me, to tell me what it needed. When the black was laid down, my initial reaction was that many of my possibilities were gone, buried in this darkness. I could not move freely; there was no lyricism here, nothing pretty to attract me—only a silent, soft atmosphere, which seemed to have no surface.

My first thought when I was asked to speak about this painting was my remembrance of the day I cut it up in small squares. The blackness was so endless that I began to intuitively feel around in the dark for ways to deal with what I felt to be the all-encompassing, absorbing, seductive, and bottomless feeling of the work. So, shortly after I began, I spontaneously cut the work up into squares and began to work on the piece like a game. I would move the pieces, paint on the work as a whole, then move them again, paint again, and so on. Some days I organized the movement like a game of chess: moving first one side and then moving the other side to correspond in some way. I was reminded of Bergman's film "The Seventh Seal" in which the knight is playing chess with Death, as I was playing a deep game with my own inner figures and experiences of death. This painting is quite large, and the physical movement required to continually move the pieces around seemed as well a way of surviving the death grip of the black; in part, a way of allowing the blackness while at the same time keeping my earthbound movement in opposition to its pull.

Indeed, the whole of this work involves ways in which to enter the black—its softness, its fertility, its silence—without being absorbed completely. As I worked, I discovered that any addition of color to the piece had to be made very carefully. The painting appears to be totally black and white, but in fact there is a great deal of color enmeshed in the darkness. The color needed to emanate from the black and could not be

FIGURE 6

superimposed in a stilted and lively way that would jar the spirit of the work. The feeling here was that the lights could not be turned on too quickly, as there was life here that was accustomed to living in the dark and not adapted to light. My struggle was to witness this dialectic as I moved with the opposing rhythms of being pulled into the darkness—for me a rich, silent, and fertile garden as well as a velvety nothingness. As I looked hopefully for a path in the black, a multiplicity of paths began to unfold.

Instead of brightening the piece, I found that I began to add layer upon layer of black in varying textures, amplifying instead of deintensifying the darkness. I worked with paint, charcoal, and lacquer, feeling that if I multiplied the black with enough invisible edges, cutting it, texturing it, and moving it, that it would at some point reflect some light and begin to give forth a form of its own. This was my own hope buried in the darkness; that given enough space the black would cease to be a deadness and move toward being a reflective surface and a source of intensity, fertility, and power.

> I immediately became aware of Priscilla's awesome potential for despair and sadness. Yet I am equally impressed by her strength, her keen sharp intellectual lines, and the grid that offers her an anchor in spite of the black, sucking pull toward the center. In her clear straight lines lies the power of the masculine, providing an anchor that will serve her well during black storms of depression. I feel that Priscilla, the artist, has encountered the call of death and has grappled with its absorbing power. Fortunately, her ability to move, to cut up, indeed to manipulate her world, makes her a survivor, for she has learned to live by her wits and has won a victory over despair. These skills underlie her ability to

mobilize aggression in the service of the self, for we observe the boundaries of self and other in spite of the powerful regressive pulls.

The texture and fabric of her work is soft and sensuous, indicating a tactile sensitivity that spills over into a passion, and an intuitive grasp of her environment. This power becomes reinforced by a capacity to merge black power into an affective relatedness to her surroundings. Perhaps this becomes a living heritage of the positive aspects of the mother-child relationship. At the same time, the structuring influences of this relationship seem poorly defined, creating the potential for Priscilla to fall into deep dark holes. As an analyst, I would be aware that this possibility may arise in treatment, which in turn, would call for a clear, articulated response on my part.

As I review this dialogue, I am reminded that if we as therapists can help our patients to remain with their blackness and depression, a new order can emerge that has its own organic integrity and power. This process cannot be rushed. Priscilla's moving statement echoes in my mind. "We must let the light in slowly." Being with a patient's blackness, not being frightened by it, or, more importantly, absorbed by it, creates the climate where wounds and losses are recognized as real and irreversible and only then are we ready to find the light of another that can guide us out of the despair. This light, of an inward and/or outward other, however dimly perceived, becomes the source of hope and transcendence. It may well explain why so many of our deprived patients seek out spiritual communities, such as Alcoholics Anonymous, that provide a light or luminosity where the black spot now lives, moves, and becomes transformed into hope and transcendence.

The dialectic between blackness and luminosity

can reach a feverish pitch, particularly in the lives of
artists who are struggling between death and existence. Michael Eigen (1986), an analyst noted for his
penetrating insights into psychosis, comments about
van Gogh's last work:

> In his last works, it is hard to say whether darkness
> devoured the light or vice versa. They fuse in a desper-
> ate, macabre way somewhere between madness and
> death. If his final paintings express, ward off, and fly in
> the face of madness, they are also death masks. The
> death that appears in them is an illuminated blackness.
> Death shines. It absorbs and becomes part of the mad-
> ness. It is impossible to say whether death absorbs mad-
> ness or madness absorbs death. These paintings are the
> face of death and what shines on this face is madness.

From a clinical perspective, my female patient of 20
years ago, presented in Chapter 3 dealing with ego
rhythm, comes to mind. Recall the transformation she
underwent in moving into her "deep black hole" of pain
and despair and finally up and out of it to become a
vibrant, vital, and solid personality. For her, bouncing
back and forth between her black sadness and her defensive acting out with men in bars becomes not only a
distraction from depression, but also a vehicle to reexperience the empty black-gray states of her childhood.
Her need to survive and deny her blackness through
sexual gaiety became affirmed in the process; but in it
was an implicit understanding that pain must be di-
luted with moments of joy, and also that erotic distraction could give new juice and energy to her state of
blackness. To undercut this mixture of sad gaiety could
only rob her of the varying empathic holding environments so necessary for the healing of the black void.
Clearly, the notion of mirroring takes on new meanings

as we encourage the creation and enlargement of dimensionality in the transitional space, thereby forming a variety of holding environments. The theme "through a glass darkly" becomes the motif of treatment intervention as we play back to our patients our empathic reflections of the different states of affect blackness. In this playback, we mirror the complex divisions of our patients' blackness and our respect of their survival mechanisms, as well as their capacity to discover the complex potential solutions enmeshed in sadness and emptiness. This enables them ultimately to forge their own meaning and free their power for creative use.

Thus, in the treatment of each patient's blackness, a unique holding rhythm must evolve emphasizing the hidden order of the depression that demands a variety of different amplifications and resonations. For instance, the heavy depressed black of one patient may require a quiet solitude by an enjoining therapist. In other instances, the therapist's white space, or schizoidness, may be a very appropriate balance to the patient's blackness. By contrast, a patient's grayness may fly off in many directions, demanding a firm order, or structure, in which the despair can rest. Still others respond to a quiet, serious intensity, or a wistful type of humor, or perhaps a clear interpretation, as the therapist becomes an open container that neither presses nor constrains the blackness, allowing the individual particles of despair to congeal into a new-found order. Depression and despair, then, require a sensitive tuning on the part of the therapist to particular nuances and intonations. Each blackness requires a unique aesthetic understanding.

In Priscilla's discussion of finding a strong source

of "aliveness" inside her which ultimately helped her master death, the important implications for therapy are evident. Aesthetically, she alludes to "intimations of a source of light," and clearly the luminous juxtaposition of black and white and shading is central to her work. The artist may come very close to another level of existence, one where the inner light transcends the boundaries of one's personal existence and where the soul, the mind, and the body become one. Spirituality, then, from an artistic perspective, may be that inner light or vision that heals and is beyond the limitation of verbal description. Transcending blackness via a spiritual connection and the creation of luminous light may offer the balance to despair and void.

In a later chapter, I will review a therapist's work with an AIDS patient where the state of transcendence becomes the missing link that transforms undeniable pain into hope and forgiveness. Borrowing from the aesthetic language again, we find no quality or room for any luminosity or for the rich interplay of black and white, as we observed in Priscilla's work. For this patient there is yet another face of blackness: rage. While the patient is in touch with the despair at the time of presentation, the patient's intense rage at the therapist/parent/society/God and the vision of forgiveness may offer a means to discover light out of his state of dark despair. Here, aggression has an enormous power that can either sink one into depression or move one forward into life.

The three schizoid patients referred to in the following chapter further reflect the working through of the multiple faces of blackness to new levels of integration. For Jan, the patient who was running from her

mother's judgmental, prying eyes, and who found solace and union in the Jewish community, her drawings
reflected graphically how "whiteness" became a void
into which she could fade away. While her spirituality
was a strong, retaining force in her life, it also served as
a defense against acknowledging or looking at the black
spots within her. Without this, there is no energy to
mobilize change. Treatment then was directed at redis-
covering pain, rage, and disappointment with another;
yet it was balanced by a sensitive understanding of
how her whiteness defended against further intrusion
and invasion by others. For Rebecca, the Ph.D. student,
who seemed to hold on to life with a thin thread,
whiteness served a very different purpose. Where
white meant transcendence for Priscilla and Jan, white
for Rebecca became emptiness. Like Jan, Rebecca runs
from her black spot, or dark side, but unlike Jan, who
escapes in her spiritual world, Rebecca simply disap-
pears into a void or frantic numbing activity. Finally,
there is Bob, the tightly restricted artist, who became
obsessional whenever he tried to express the anger that
was pitted against loss. His drawings of himself were
composed of fuzzy black lines defining the upper section, while the lower part of his body faded out into
white nothingness. Here, white indicated a lack of so-
lidity or internal structure rather than spirituality or
transcendence. Again there was the need for solid, firm
black lines to balance the nothingness of white; the
owning and accessing of dark, aggressive, sexual energy to give the push for reaching out to life.

Should you, the reader, entertain the possibility of
a personal exploration into the dimensions of blackness, you might want to try this exercise that was pre-

sented in many countries and different parts of the United States: I requested the participants to take a black crayon and permit themselves to scribble black lines without attempting to control the form on a white sheet of paper; to simply allow the rhythm of the lines or forms to emerge. Then I requested the members of the workshop to find the hidden order of the blackness and to amplify the blackness into a creative expression of themselves; in other words, into a work of art. Then, something very interesting happened. A few of the students ripped up the paper until you couldn't discern the blackness at all. Others put so much color around it that the black was disguised. A few said to me that they wanted to build on the black, but were ashamed of others seeing it. Others spoke about the white part of the drawing and said it wasn't the black part that scared them but the whiteness, or emptiness.

If generalizations could be made, and admittedly they are sketchy at this time, I found the Swiss students making powerful, organic dark lines to the center of their dark self. They did, indeed, seem very comfortable with blackness, like an old friend. On the other hand the Italians transformed their blackness into soft sensuous vibrations, sometimes rhythmic; in other instances it came close to fuzziness. The Swedes, though not frightened of the blackness, gave it color and humor, almost like alternation in rhythm and movement.

It seems to me that all these observations say something important as to how we work with depression and schizoid phenomena. Too often, we as therapists either miss the multiple dimensions of these states or else try to impose an order rather than encourage our patients to feel the very heart of blackness—to discover their own particular sense of blackness. Clearly, black is not simply black. Making use of an aesthetic sensibility and language offers a rich framework within which to approach "black" states.

6

The Psychoaesthetics of the Real and Transference Relationships in the Treatment of Schizoid Phenomena

In the therapeutic communicative structure, the expression of the aesthetic takes place both within the transference and countertransference relationship as well as the real relationship. These two levels of communication can either complement, mirror, or oppose one another, but the mode of interaction must be understood in order to facilitate appropriate treatment interventions. In treatment, the art form of the patient is expressed through transference and represents an attempt to master pain, albeit the aesthetics are skewed and distorted. Each transference expression that evolves in treatment presents its own particular pattern

This chapter is based upon Robbins, Arthur (1988). The interface of the real and transference relationships in schizoid phenomena. *Psychoanalytic Review*, 75, 393–418.

of aesthetic organization with its potential for transformations that are reshaped in an ongoing treatment
process. We refer back to Rose's (1987) important contribution to this text. Rose acknowledges the importance
of the internalization process that transpires between
patient and therapist as an important facilitator in treatment. The facilitation of this internalization process becomes an art form in and of itself. Most important, this
identification process is not confined to patients who
exhibit primitive mental states. We cite once again the
significant work by Behrends and Blatt (1985, p. 213),
that emphasizes that internalization evolves in a climate
of both frustration and gratification. Internalization occurs when interactions that have been formerly gratifying are interrupted. Thus, in order to regain a trace of
the gratifying experience, an identification with the
previously gratifying object must take place. The sym-
bolization of the therapist and the internalization of his
presence then becomes an important anchor and organizer that facilitates the assimilation of insight. Without
this anchor, insight is not integrated within the self, but
becomes part of the patient's intellectualized defenses.
Most important, this new internalization gives permission to the patient to provide a climate where they can
rediscover their own internal rhythm. Consequently,
the importance of developing a transitional space between patient and therapist cannot be overemphasized
in facilitating an identification process. We view gratification as the furthering of a deep mutual oneness between patient and therapist, reminiscent of both the
artist merging with his medium in one phase of creation and the primary creativity of mother and child. In
therapy, this feeling of oneness and deep resonance is

channeled through the intonation of voice, postural and facial expressions, and kinesthetic resonance which are manifestations of the primary process and which in turn fuel the whole movement of treatment. In short, without this attunement, there is no juice going on in treatment.

Frustration arises in the form of separateness and the disrupting of this resonance with interpretive interventions. The artistry of the therapist is in evidence when she introduces appropriate pacing of different forms of interpretations that inevitably interferes with this early resonance. Yet, in a climate of good enough mothering, the patient does internalize a connecting symbolic link associated with the therapist and utilizes this image as a stabilizing center for the assimilation and organization of insight. As with any dual level of consciousness, new forms are constantly being developed that are basically facilitated through a very elastic notion of transitional space. Without the sensitive employment and responsiveness to the shifting needs of transitional space within the relationship, this identification process becomes disrupted. Furthermore, this resonance changes as it responds to a new emerging aesthetic form from the transference. Along the same lines, the identification process may be equally impaired if we do not offer shape and structure to the transitional space. Form, then, through the medium of interventions includes verbal interpretations and an adherence to the psychotherapeutic frame. Therefore, an essential aesthetic of treatment revolves around the interplay of nonverbal resonance and interpretive form. This appropriate mix of frustration and gratification and/or form and resonance will be contingent on such

factors as the patient's ego defenses and self–object organizations that are associated with a particular transferential phase of treatment. Therapeutic artistry then
becomes contingent on the therapist's receptivity to a
variety of different energies expressed on a number of
psychic levels which in turn must be responded to with
different types of holding environments and interpretive forms. In short, the structure that is created in both
nonverbal and verbal expression, such as how loose or
tight, distant or far, will be crucial in creating and furthering this identification process.

Transference manifestations are examples of creativity gone wrong. As was presented in Chapter 3, the
creative spirit of an individual lives and breathes
through a sensitive attunement to an internal rhythm
of oscillation between form and formlessness of intrapsychic energy. In this movement, a cycle of birth, life,
death, and regeneration are part of giving old forms
new meaning as our very identity style changes with
life circumstances. Transference, albeit a creative expression of the patient, usually ends up in a repetitious
organization of psychic space. In short, the aesthetic is
incomplete and does not set the stage for the oscillation
of form and formlessness. For patients, then, their internal transitions of psychic energy are either absent or
confined to a very limited area of life. For example, a
patient may permit his/her creative force to exist in
work, while the interpersonal sphere remains stale and
limited. The real relationship that manifests itself in
treatment becomes an important counterbalance that
gradually metabolizes and reorganizes the transference
and offers a new internalization of therapeutic presence
to take place that encourages the regeneration of an
ego rhythm.

Thus, in treatment, we see two art forms in play: one very incomplete, which occurs in transference, and the other more open and accessible, which occurs in the real relationship. In treatment, we are constantly playing with psychic art diptychs. Here, we mirror, complement, or even oppose the psychoaesthetic organization of the transference. This may occur on a nonverbal level and is largely expressed through the style of therapeutic contact. The purpose, however, of the real relationship is to open up the closed system of the transference so that what was previously an incomplete art form of the transference now finds new energy and form from the real relationship.

Schizoid phenomena in which patients exhibit a hunger for the real relationship offer an excellent example of the interplay of the psychoaesthetics of transference being played out within the larger context of a psychoaesthetic form. This will be amplified in an article that was previously entitled, "The Interface of the Real and Transference Relationship in the Treatment of Schizoid Phenomena" (Robbins, 1988).

By way of an introduction, I would like to share with the reader a personal memory that became an organizing symbol during my personal analysis, and has no doubt influenced the development of my approach to treatment of the schizoid. I recall long hours of sitting in a big black baby carriage in the sun, tucked away from outside passing traffic. As I grew up, the carriages changed; first a black one, then a brown one, but invariably I was safely swaddled away all by myself. There are few affects or associations connected to this early memory. Later on, I do recall playing with cheese boxes that were used to construct a musical instrument.

As vividly as this memory stands out for me, and as important an image as it now seems, I had little to say about this experience during the initial phase of treatment. Basically, this phase was marked by long silences in which I feared my analyst would despair from the boredom of it all. I did share, as best I could, my experience of mother. She was responsible, but was all too contained inside herself, wrapped up with fits of depression. She simply was not "present" with her children. She did attempt to do the right and responsible things, and as long as I was in my carriage and was out of trouble, she was content to go on and occupy herself with her various household duties. Indeed, I am sure she thought there could be no better life for a growing baby than to be basking in the sun like a turtle on a log, safe and protected from any harm or danger. I do not recall many memories of my mother or father reading to me, and in fact, this may have had some bearing on an early reading disability.

As I approached analysis, I felt there was very little for me to say about my life. Everything seemed all right: my marriage was fine and I was earning a living. My one reservation was to wonder whether I belonged in the analytic profession, but I could not elaborate on this problem except in a rather flat cursory tone. I simply doubted if I had much to give my patients. In spite of my seeming lack of material, I was somehow relieved that analysis was a required part of analytic training.

During this early period when there were many lengthy empty silences in which I had little sense of what to say or how to communicate my feelings regarding my life history, fortunately my analyst did not desert me. Sometimes he would offer me "bedtime stories" in the form of citing plays, literature, and movies that had some relevance to the diffuse threads and images I presented to him in treatment. My curiosity was aroused by the references and I made a point of reading the material. The likes of Ibsen, Dostoyevski, and Kafka became important sources of rich symbolic material that seemed to mirror and clarify my inner experiences. Literature, and later art, seemed to give symbolic form to what I was trying to express. Most importantly, this material became a significant means to sharing emotionally with my analyst.

During the course of analysis, I feared that I was receiving supportive treatment rather than "real" analysis. It was later on, after my analysis was over, that I started to review this experience. Only then did I understand the significance of the sharing in my own treatment.

I remember my first consultation with a different analyst. He was rather passive and quiet. I recall how he would stare at me as I stumbled around trying to tell him why I was there. After this initial consultation, I wondered if I had the strength to endure treatment. "If this is analysis," I said to myself, "the isolation is more than I can bear." Soon thereafter, I attempted to test myself out again with my present analyst. He was quite different: he spoke directly to me, sharing his feelings regarding my problems, and as a result I soon felt his presence in the room. This did not preclude the development of a number of transference issues that became prevalent throughout my treatment. What his sharing did do was to make contact with me and address my profound sense of aloneness. It is the working with this "schizoid" sense of isolation and blankness through the juxtaposition of the real and transference relationships that I wish to address in this chapter.

Emotional states of isolation and emptiness can be observed in any number of different character structures organized with a variety of defenses from hysterics and obsessionals to depressives or borderlines, but most typically in schizoid disorders. In the latter, we find both dread and resignation as responses to being alone, as well as an underlying wish and fear to make contact with the interpersonal world. Aloneness, therefore, becomes a fortress against the world, while also serving as an isolating prison. Pockets of this profound aloneness and dissociation can be found in all of us regardless of the specific character armor we wear or the unique family history we carry with us (Guntrip, 1971). For instance, it can be seen in the frantic hunger for activities that masks a fear of any real relatedness. We can see how professionals fill in their busy schedules to avoid feelings of nothingness or how some artists make contact with the world mainly through their personal creative work while remaining severely limited in their interpersonal life. Here, the art form, be it fine or applied, becomes a personal invitation to the audience to see and hear, but also a means of maintaining a safe distance from the artist. The art form then serves as a connecting link to interpersonal survival.

The genesis of the schizoid position as described in the literature differs among theoreticians. Althea Horner (1979) refers to the schizoid conditions as a variation of borderline development manifested by a denial of a state of incomplete and unworked-through symbiosis. The self is buried in a blanked-out cloud as a means to avoid the pain associated with the original problems of attachment. Within this framework, the therapeutic approach is one of directing and uncovering the original symbiotic pain and then working through both the integration of good and bad, as well as the underlying dread of ambivalence.

By contrast, Giovacchini (1979) views the schizoid disorder as a fixation of the prementational level and associates it with related deficiencies in cognitive structures and secondary-process organization. These problems are traced to difficulties in the attachment level connected with a deficiency in internalizing a functional introject. Without this very basic underpinning to the personality structure, an individual lacks the anchor that is so necessary to build adequate ego functions. Obviously, if no symbiosis existed, an individual would die; so enough introjection for basic living has occurred in the schizoid individual. The relative lack of this functional introject, however, is evidenced in an inadequate bridge from the inside mental state to the outside interpersonal world. Horner, I believe, would contend that such a condition would lead to the development of a basically psychopathological individual with a cold ruthless approach to a nonsupportive and unnurturing world. Here, then, we see an important diagnostic dimension to this problem of the schizoid phenomena: Do feelings of emptiness relate to early attachment issues or are they associated with denial and a fear of relationships? Giovacchini's approach to schizoid dynamics reflects Guntrip's (1971) theoretical position. To quote the latter:

> The fundamental cause of the development of a schizoid condition is the experience of isolation resulting from the loss of mental rapport with the mother, at a time

> when the mother is the baby's sole environment and the
> whole world, so that he has no alternate defense.

Most important, as was stated previously, Guntrip emphasizes that schizoid phenomena appear in a variety of characterological organizations and represents the rock-bottom core of analytic treatment.

Regardless of the ultimate genesis of this problem, in therapy one of the underlying missions in working with schizoid phenomena is to help patients develop skills and attitudes that relate to making the inside reality an outside possibility. Yet by definition, a patient who has strongly entrenched schizoid features lacks the desire to make the inside an outside reality. We are then challenged as therapists to enter the world of "the void" and/or blackness where fantasies and symbols are but vague structures, often buried within the body, and where actions are disconnected from the patient's conscious awareness of self. This state of aloneness reflects an obliviousness to society's demands and conventions. Thus, in contrast to the psychopathic individual, these patients are not driven by power motives as much as by feelings of contempt or disinterest toward society's rules and conventions. They simply go their own way, often oblivious to what it takes to win societal approval. This disinterest in convention and conformity becomes the theme of the schizoid's existence. In treatment, we can hear the refrain, "Nothing was given to me, so why should I care what society has to offer?" If anything, society becomes an intrusion that at best can be met with denial, withdrawal, or dissociation. The therapist, then, as an agent of society, rebuilds the transitional space where meaning and action become congruent with one another.

For the schizoid individual, the therapeutic transitional space becomes a "place" where he can rediscover or discover what relatedness means through the regeneration of primary creativity and the need to reorder and redefine energy arising out of this process. In this analytic dyad, it is the analyst's reservoir of symbols, images, and nonverbal responsiveness that becomes the basis for the recreation and regeneration of the analytic transitional space.

In order to elaborate on the interrelations of the psychoaesthetics of the real and transference relationships, fragments of three cases will be discussed. The three patients are characterologically different in nature, but with underlying features of the schizoid phenomena.* In each case, the aspect of the transference–countertransference relationship can be characterized by a similar induction. Simply stated, "Come close for I am alone, but stay away for I fear intrusion." There are also feelings regarding the wish to have an impact on the therapist as well as being unworthy of such intimacy.

The cases that will be discussed represent different developmental deficiencies and problems and a variety of defenses and internalized object relations. Yet, all three patients suffer to some extent from a sense of aloneness, or according to Winnicott, "a deficiency in ego relatedness." Here we will see problems in organizing inner thoughts, affects, and perceptions in relationship to another being. Each of the three patients introduce into treatment a similar complaint: "I don't

---

*Parts of these three cases have been reported in a different context in Robbins, Arthur (1987). *The artist as therapist*. New York: Human Sciences Press.

know why I'm here, but I feel alone and am frightened."

While each of these patients have friends and are competent in their work, there is always the expression of an inner feeling of being alone. Let's proceed with the first case.

Doris, age 38, had been in treatment at different points in her life with three different therapists for a total of seven years. As she entered my consultation office, I observed panic and fear in her eyes. She tensely sat in her chair like a cat ready to spring. Her eyes darted back and forth, feeling out the territory, venturing only slowly and tentatively into relating with me. She continued to scan every corner of my office, fearfully sensing out danger as she told me her story. She was a psychology intern in a Ph.D. program and was frightened that she would do something terrible to her patients. "I don't know what's happening," she said, in a terrified voice. Interestingly, her fieldwork reports were positive and her grades were very good, but still there was panic in her voice regarding her work.

As she started to tell me her story, her physical movements said more to me than her words. As she spoke, she rocked back and forth in her chair trying to offer herself some form of self-soothing. I felt something ominous and frightening in the room, but I wasn't quite sure if it was me or some vague, frightening presence.

As treatment progressed, in spite of her helplessness and suspicions, she did find support and care in our relationship. She completed graduate school and obtained a job in a local mental health clinic. Predictably, her case load was full of borderline patients, all of whom catalyzed her into one crisis state or another. While her patients were seemingly driving her crazy with their acting out, the excitement of borderline dynamics seemed to affectively engage her, for she had an intuitive feel for working with this type of diagnosis. These patients and her reactions to them were the subject of much discussion. As she spoke of her work, I avoided giving specific advice, and learned a good deal about her feelings through these cases. In the process, she started to tell me her life story. She described her mother as a narcissistically depressed, occasionally violent woman who presented a social veneer of friendliness to the world. As she described her, I thought of the film, "Mommie Dearest," and I recommended that Doris see it. The next session, after seeing the film, she came in and cried out, "Joan Crawford is my mother. She is exactly like that. On the surface she is warm and even gracious and sociable, but inside, there is a killer who demands absolute obedience." There was a mutual feeling of excitement that became part of our interaction. Through the metaphor of Joan Crawford, both of us felt that we had a better understanding of this maternal demon.

As our treatment progressed, a crucial transference issue emerged. She was unable to feel my presence in the room. Although I shared a good deal of myself, she still complained of my being unavailable. I recall speaking to her in soft, fond tones. My voice was quiet but intense, mirroring on the one hand, complementing on the other, this terrible sense of fear pervading the atmosphere. Her mother's presence seemed continuously to be interjected into our relationship. When I temporarily left for a vacation, Doris went into a state of terror, and her supervisor took over quasi-ther-apeutic duties. Doris maintained she required a whole team of therapists, for how could she trust her life to simply one human being? Therapy with one therapist was too much for her to endure. When I returned from the vacation, I became aware that my words seemed to be bouncing off her, making little contact. The terror of being in the same room with "Mommie Dearest" seemed to surround us. The patient at times was liter-ally in mortal fear for her life. In time, these vague, unknown attacks seemed to abate, coming out of a reestablishing of a quiet, but intense presence with my patient.

From time to time, I invited her to draw. She re-sponded positively to this approach and felt that draw-ing spoke to her more strongly than words. "All those words are words," she reported, "and all I hear at times, is 'bla-bla-bla.' I don't know what you're talking about." My rationale for using drawings was based on the developmental premise that a good deal of my pa-tient's life existed on a nonverbal level. Gestures and tactile responses were more meaningful than second-ary-process thinking. I also thought that the playful in-terchange that went on in the drawing would foster a mother–child-like relationship. I did need to keep in mind that enclosing this very immature and unde-veloped self, however, was a functioning ego that helped her to navigate in the world. Perhaps the outer social veneer of the mother was internalized, creating an important bridge between herself and others.

About a year into treatment, the patient continued to complain about my lack of presence. In response, I suggested, "Let's draw me and you right now." She was very pleased by this suggestion and immediately went to work. As she started to draw, she said: "This is my father. I am on the outside holding him together, yet, I am also in the inside following him along the outside perimeter." Then she drew a little dot on the outside and said, "You know, I can't be on the outside because I'll get killed, so this is me on the outside, the small dot. I am holding my father. Yet, I am only a reflection of the outside. As I am holding my father on the outside, I am also on the inside—my father is here with a big mouth. I cannot exist alone, but I cannot let anybody inside me. I can only exist by hiding in somebody else" (Figure 7).

Soon after this session, we started to explore her feelings about women. She drew a picture of mother and saw a picture of a female with no feet and jagged hands. There were scars on the face and wounds on the hands and the eyes. The patient amplified the power of the drawing by commenting that her mother attempted suicide when her own mother died while Doris was in her early adolescence. I responded in a tone that communicated intense concern and involvement. We had in front of us a graphic portrayal of "Mommie Dearest" (Figure 8). The patient, however, could offer very few associations regarding the mother except what she already had shared with me.

Then a new secret was divulged. "She has inside her a person named Tom. If you don't know who Tom is, Tom is very important. He protects me and gives me comfort." We joked about Tom and welcomed a new member into our treatment relationship. I then asked her if she would talk about the male and female inside her. Doris saw herself as heterosexual, but basically felt

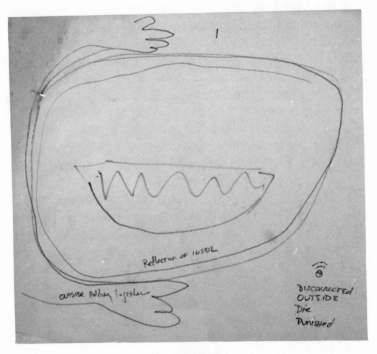

FIGURE 7

FIGURE 8

like a male. This prompted me to ask her to draw a picture of both the male and female inside herself. My attention was drawn toward both faces, a most important contact point between mother and child. It was striking how empty these faces appeared, as if the mirror had been broken. The female had no hands with which to touch or facial features with which to implement contact in the world. There was also minimal sexual differentiation (Figure 9). When Doris then drew Tom, a far more intact and cohesive image emerged (Figure 10).

Another picture soon came up as our discussion turned to femininity. Doris shared with me her feelings about Tina Turner, a rock singer, "a black primitive woman with a deep soul" and a tough edge to her. Also, of interest, she was a singer with a brutalized background. Doris collected all Turner's records and felt very connected to the woman. Even with this sense of connectedness, however, as Doris drew Tina Turner, the breasts weren't fully etched out, there were no arms, and the face was blurred, although there was the beginning of eyes and a mouth (Figure 11). It seemed that through the singer, there was a search for a female identity going on that mirrored Doris's primitive self. I proceeded to buy some of Tina Turner's records and listened to her singing, and I shared with the patient my reactions to the singer's voice.

A series of other drawings regarding crucial issues in my patient's life emerged in which we began to see signs of a cognitive structure where memories and perceptions in time and space took form. Each one of these graphic representations truly did go beyond the sphere of words. Here, then, were the beginnings of

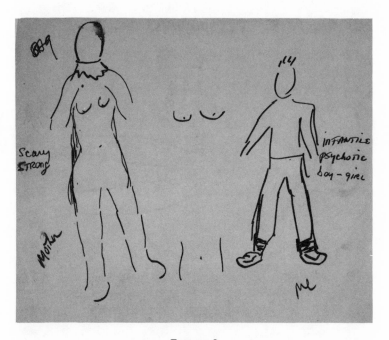

FIGURE 9

FIGURE 10

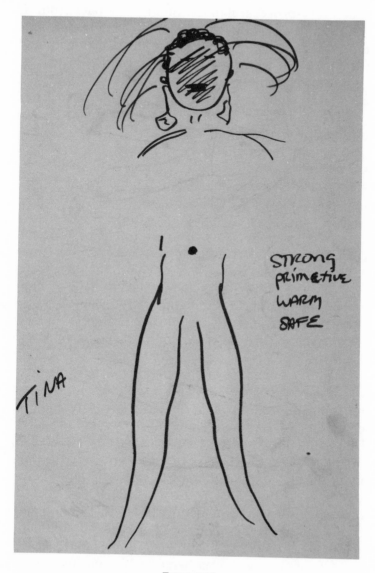

FIGURE 11

secondary-process elaboration. In the background, however, though never explicitly pointed out, was the real relationship providing a structure, mediated through clear, warm responsiveness. I felt nurturing, gentle, and very holding of this woman as I encouraged her to draw, and was enthusiastic about her responses.

I shared with Doris that I was going to present her case in Switzerland and requested her permission to use her case material. During this period of treatment she was becoming increasingly ambivalent and frightened of the growing attachment to me. I quote, "Craving you is like being hooked to a drug; there's nowhere to go." Then, as an unconscious acting out of her message, she began to sell marijuana to her professional colleagues. She received tremendous satisfaction from selling drugs, and was very happy with the service she was providing. In the session in which we talked about my presentation, she commented, "Tell your audience that I really feel it is a worthwhile service even though it is illegal and limited." I carried this message to my audience and we shared our subtle unconscious joke regarding pot. Both of us understood that we were talking about the transference. Yet it was through the real relationship that I provided a holding structure that was clear, limited, and safe enough for the exploration of Doris' growing fear and wish to make contact with and incorporate a very primitive mother. Hopefully the clarity of the image of the therapist could help Doris brave the terror of the transference, the latter being characterized as fuzzy and disorganized, with piercing and frighteningly loose energy, and with underlying menacing, jagged, cutting lines.

Of interest here was her report upon my return

from Switzerland. For the first time she was not pan-icked by my absence. In fact, she was elated and ex-cited by her reaction. She reported that at least at some point I was thinking about her, even if it was perhaps for my own selfish reasons. It seemed to be important to her that there was a mixture of both "Mommie Dear-est" and the real caring relationship represented in the presentation. Again, through the real relationship, the abandoning transference transformed itself into cogni-tive possibilities. It was action rather than a verbal in-terpretation that made its mark. Doris, psychologically without arms, legs, or eyes, received an appropriate form and structure in which to explore feelings of de-sertion, abandonment, and need.

Subsequently this paper was presented in New York, and Doris, with much trepidation, decided to at-tend the conference. Her colleague, a transference "Tom," encouraged her to attend and sat with her. In the session immediately afterward, she cheerfully re-ported how moved and touched she was by my gentle approach in discussing her material. She then pre-sented a new drawing made immediately after hearing my presentation. It was that of a 6-year-old boy called Christopher, who was "lost, fragile, and very young in-side" (Figure 12). She shared her growing feelings of love toward me and expressed fear that it might be too much of a burden for me to bear. Certainly, her mother's love was experienced as intrusive. She wanted none of that and wondered if I felt the same way. I reassured her that I truly was not her mother and was quite able to accept her love and care for me. As she related these very moving and tender feelings, she virtually wailed out and cried for the sheer pain of the material. Some

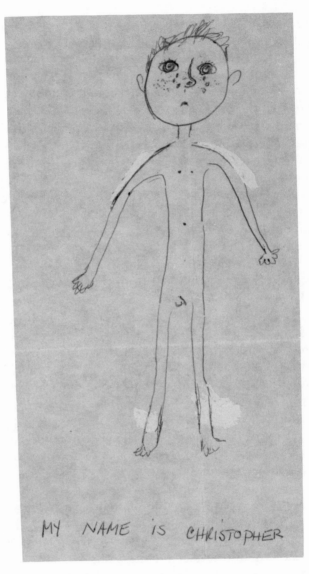

MY NAME IS CHRISTOPHER

FIGURE 12

where deep down, she said, there was another image. It was that of a very young child, perhaps a baby, who was ugly and revolting and full of sores and disease. She did not know with whom this baby could ever enter a relationship, but then brightened slightly at the thought that maybe it was already here.

Slowly, the early rejected feelings of self were brought into our relationship. I asked her to make the "sick baby" out of clay. With much distaste, she proceeded to do so and then, with a sculpting tool, cut it up and destroyed it. My interpreting that mother was now in the room made very little impact on the patient. As she destroyed the baby, however, I made a new baby and placed it on the table. It was there for her to own when she was ready to take a further step in differentiating from mother. My response communicated on two levels. On the one hand, I accepted her attachment to her harsh mother and her need to mutilate herself to maintain the attachment. I also offered the hope that there could be a regeneration of the self through a symbolic connection with the therapist. Thus, with appropriate distance as well as closeness, Doris was able to observe and understand the quality of our relationship that made it possible for her to risk sharing some very deep and tender feelings about care, mothering, closeness, and self-hate. The need for intimacy, fears of possession, and destructiveness, as well as her masochistic submission to mother, became the focus of treatment. The aesthetics of the real relationship, I believe, created the possibilities for exploration. Her potential for closeness was slowly emerging, although we still had a long journey in this direction.

I'd like to summarize the important aspects of the

psychoaesthetics of the real relationship that seemed to interface with the psychoaesthetics of the transference–countertransference. Most important were the subtle, soft tones of my voice and manner which reflected a recognition of Doris' need for mothering. This tone was in part the pulling forth of some of the internalizations that are connected with my own early mothering experiences. Perhaps a piece of me identified with her sense of aloneness. Most important, however, was the constructive use of the schizoid part of myself in treatment. This empty space was no longer a safe bastion or retreat from contact. Indeed, it was now used to scan and contain particles of my patient's primitive existence. Moving in and out of the schizoid position, then, becomes part of a creative life-giving therapeutic contact.

The introduction of art materials became a major parameter framing the real relationship. Here, the mutual playing with visual symbols, along with the introduction of a movie and records, created an important meeting space for both patient and therapist. Later, at a more advanced developmental level, her awareness that I was preparing a paper about her life in treatment became another important dimension of the real relationship, as she took some distance to get a better conceptual image of the therapist. This awareness of my emotional investment in her treatment seemed to further the attachment process. Here, as well as with other cases where attachment issues are primary, the analyst's presence and commitment become an important factor in facilitating treatment. Most important was the development of a transitional space truly felt by the patient. It was that "space" that allowed her to face some of the archaic representations of her past.

The second clinical example will describe a very different use of the real relationship that facilitates transference–countertransference communications. I first saw Joan 20 years ago for a period of 3 years where a significant amount of time was devoted to her preoccupation with her Arab lover. I recall my first impressions of her: lonely, with deep soulful eyes and an erotic quality that filled the office. I thought immediately to myself, "This is the woman from the picture 'Hiroshima Mon Amour.' " I recalled the female role in this picture and how her personal life mirrored the destructiveness, fragmentation, and chaos of a nuclear disaster. The sharing of this picture with my patient became an important organizing influence upon her whole life history.

As the patient told me about her life, she described her mother as a very busy woman who was almost exclusively preoccupied with running a dry-goods store. As a baby, Joan would stay for long hours in the back room while her parents worked in the front part of the shop. She recalled her room as being dark and gloomy. Nevertheless, she was a good child and complained very little. While Joan's mother was unavailable, her father, on the other hand, was soft but nonverbal and she received a good deal of physically close contact with him. Rarely did she feel that either parent really understood her. She experienced her mother as a steamroller. Joan simply could not argue or discuss anything with her as she rushed by to do her work. Being a strongly opinionated woman, she was invariably intractable in her attitudes and responses to her daughter's wishes and needs.

The patient's preoccupation was with a love affair,

doomed before it began. He was an Arab; she a Jew. She tried to extricate herself from the relationship, but was caught in a stickiness of hate, love, and provocation. Her affair was like a drug, making her feel dependent and unfulfilled. She challenged, placated, and was enraged, but the relationship seemed to go nowhere. She could not leave her lover, but knew that the external constraints of her lover's work precluded any real resolution to their love affair. He was a diplomat and she was unacceptable in his society. The relationship finally terminated and her lover left for Iran. As the patient grappled with her gloom and abandonment, she resolved to find more meaning in her life and decided to move to Israel. Her parents, emigrants, fled from Nazi prosecution and wandered from one country to another until they landed in America. In the United States, Joan never felt part of the culture and saw New York as a cold and lonely place. Israel, she felt, would be more related and community oriented. Perhaps there she could find a new life. While she recognized that she was trying to find an external solution for her inside problems, she also felt she had been in treatment long enough.

Joan stayed in Israel for fifteen years, and then one day I received a call with a very familiar voice at the other end. "I am back from Israel and I want to start treatment again." Although unstated, I also heard an elusive quality of speaking that communicated, "I am lonely and sad, hold me, touch me." During our first session, I again felt the familiar unrelatedness as Joan spoke about her problems in most vague terms. It seemed she had gone from one love affair to another, all of which were rather unfulfilling. Only when she spoke of Israel, did she become truly alive.

Two years into treatment, the familiar problems of unrelatedness continued to plague us. We were both aware of the problem, but seemingly were unable to do too much about it. After a series of rather disconnected sessions, I said to her, "Why not draw what is happening between us."

"No, no, I could never capture what is going on," Joan protested. She didn't like to draw; this was not her metaphor. Movement and touch were where she lived, yet reluctantly, she was willing to take a chance and draw.

After drawing her first picture she said, "See, I told you. Look how bad it is. That's you and that's me, and I am missing so many things. The facial expression, there's nothing there, and the warmth of my eyes is absent. My strength isn't there. Even my fear of passivity or receptivity are absent" (Figure 13).

I said, "Why not correct it? How about putting those in?"

"I won't be able to do it," she lamented.

"Go ahead," I encouraged. "Try it."

I was aware that my patient required a good deal of encouragement. My choice was to either analyze the resistance or follow my intuition. I followed the latter and she proceeded to complete the drawings (Figure 14). As she looked at her finished pictures, she said, "Now I feel somewhat better. Again the mouth is missing, but at least it is stronger, it's more defined and it says who I am." She said it had a kind of "animacy," and added, "I don't know if that's the right word." She meant adamant, but in calling it "animacy" perhaps she was thinking of a combination of "adamant" and "mimicry." She felt more grown up as she described her

FIGURE 13

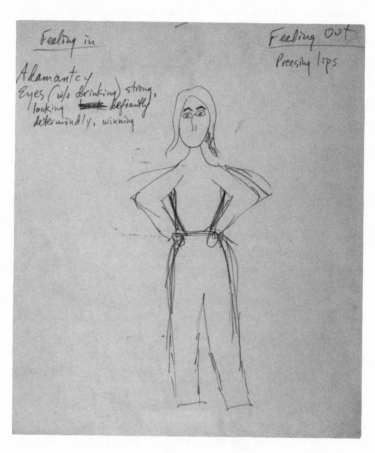

FIGURE 14

second drawings. Again, though, I noted the drawing seemed to be floating in air. They weren't really grounded, yet there was something more defiant and present to her images than before. Then suddenly out of nowhere I felt the energy diminish in the room. The room seemed to go blank, and I commented that I felt disconnected as she moved far away.

"What happened?" I asked.

She agreed that she was aware that something was going on, and said, "I know we are losing contact with one another, but I don't know what to do."

I asked her to draw what was going on, and the next picture emerged (Figure 15). In commenting on it, she said: "One third of it is you and two thirds of it is me. You know, my mother was a very demanding woman. She was very intrusive and controlling, and I learned that the only way I could win an argument was by shutting up and going my own way. That was the only way I survived. I let her yell and scream, and just shrugged my shoulders."

I saw, now, that a piece of the transference was becoming clearer for both of us. I recognized that perhaps I was being too intrusive, and I wondered about this aloud. She denied this, but stayed angry, maintaining that she really didn't like anyone getting too close to her. The transference and the associated defense were played out as the obstinate, negative girl came out from hiding. Through the visual metaphor I heard, "Try and make me. I'm not going to do what you want, so you can push all you want."

This insight permitted a more active contact as well as increased openness by my patient. We spent a good deal of time talking about Zionism. Joan was appalled

FIGURE 15

about my stand regarding Israel. She tried to convert me to her point of view. She was very angry that I did not identify with Israeli causes.

"What kind of a Jew are you?" she'd demand.

I shared with her some of my feelings about Judaism, and we had an active discussion about the meaning of Jewishness. "You're not a Jew at all. Don't you know that you cannot separate Judaism from Israel?" she strongly stated. I knew she was somehow picking up a crucial and subtle issue in my own identity as a Jew. The identification between analyst and patient took the form of the patient telling the analyst, "Don't be alienated like me." Of further importance, the powerful mother was present in our relationship. This time, however, neither one of us felt overwhelmed. Introject mother and lost little girl came out of hiding and a very active discussion of Judaism and "the mother homeland" ensued. The once-rejected Jewish spirit that had been acted out, I believe, via the love affair with the Arab diplomat now was a point of self-affirmation in transference–countertransference discussion.

Once again, the message transmitted through the real relationship rather than interpretation started the process of neutralization of the overwhelmed child and powerful mother within the patient. Through the real relationship, new structures merged that increased the patient's ability to develop secondary-process functioning. Through sharing and labeling her feelings, the patient learned that opposition and differences did not mean the annihilation of the self. My active sharing regarding Israel and Judaism became the format through which to work through self–object differentiation and secondary-process structuralization.

Upon review of this very short presentation, I am aware that the playful, nonverbal symbolic contact was equally an important factor in facilitating the unfolding of transference material. In contrast to the first case, however, there was a mixture of softness and spirited interchange that characterized our dialogues. The early attachment problem did not seem as pronounced in Joan as with Doris, and there seemed to be a more important need to practice and separate. Consequently there was less "symbiotic-like" relatedness and much more a testing out of Joan's own strength that characterized our treatment contact. The aesthetic of the real relationship was flexible, soft, but very clear, with energy that reached out, but did not easily expand; the patient's aesthetic was bubbly, light, purple, and playful, like a Klee painting.

The third clinical vignette elaborates on the phenomenon of loneliness and isolation found within a very different personality structure. George came to me after being in bioenergetic therapy for 4 years for his back problem. He was constantly in pain despite numerous medical attempts to ameliorate his problems. My suspicion was that the peripheral symptoms masked conflicts of isolation, fears and wishes of emotional support, unfulfilled relationships with women, minimal contacts with friends, and dissatisfaction with work.

George, reared in an upper-middle-class family consisting of nine children, lived in a very small town in Michigan. Being Jewish, he felt isolated from the mainstream Christian community, but this isolation was only a further extension of his life with his family. The mother, a very busy woman, assisted her dentist husband and raised nine children. The family mythos was one of success, competency, and adequacy. All the children abided by this credo and became either doctors or professionals with the exception of George. He complained to me with much pain, "I cannot follow my father's life which I find empty and shallow, yet I cannot find a permission inside myself to go anywhere else."

The only way to make contact with mother was being her helper. For George, this was translated on the emotional level as the assumption that men were exploited by women. On the other hand, he felt unable to compete with men, and removed himself from situations that demanded a competitive stance. In short, George was seen as a failure in his family, not having the right stuff to start his own family and become a success.

George earned his living as a carpenter and enjoyed working with his hands. Through a friend, he learned I was an art therapy teacher at Pratt Institute and, among other things, he noticed my son's paintings on the office wall. He was intrigued with the big splashy quality as contrasted to his tight, constricted style of painting. In treatment, we spent many sessions talking about the creative process, artistic expression, and their ingredients, such as loss of control, and playing with personal images. Through our discussion, an old love affair was rekindled, and George started to paint. This identification process became amplified as his feminine receptive part was now affirmed by his therapist. This positive affirmation of the patient was not forthcoming from the father, and this vehicle permitted the patient to look at his relationships with women.

Let us take a look as to how this process evolved. George needed to control everything, and his perfectionism and obsessiveness bound him into tight, somatic knots. He didn't make much money through his work, for he charged too little and invested too much of himself in any one job. His emotional knots seemed to parallel his physical complaints. In spite of all the exercises and bioenergetic therapy, there was still much pain coming from his back. I encouraged him to spend more time in his painting and drawing. Interestingly, his back symptoms started to abate. He became looser and freer in taking chances with his artwork, and a sense of excitement grew as he started to experience and work with greater freedom and personal involvement. In encouraging George to follow the exploration of his artwork, I perceived that he was also tapping an authentic piece of self-expression. I knew that this man had received little support in following his own path. The psychoaesthetic of the transference was one of pained, heavy, black deadness. The aesthetic of the real relationship was light, warm, open, and yet clear and structured, round and also pointed.

Here my encouragement as well as my interest in the creative process and painting seemed to offer an extremely important frame within which we made contact. My summer break during our first year of treatment came all too soon. I was away for two months and in September George's symptoms returned. I asked him if he could visualize what was in his back and he reported the presence of an embryo.

"Do you think that you can get some support for this embryo?" I asked.

"From you?" he complained, "You who go away for

two months! Can I depend on you when you go away?
Things were going along very nicely until you decided
to take a vacation." He was bitter and angry. I encouraged him to draw his feelings about our relationship
when he returned to his studio. "Perhaps," he said, but
he was reluctant to give me anything. He then brought
in a series of three drawings describing his feelings
about our relationship. The first one had to do "with me
and you." "This is you trying to hold me," he said.
"You're just like my entire family: I am bound, separated. I am apart from you. There you are, and this is
me. I am on my knees, you are sitting out there and we
can never make contact. It is like my whole family. In
treatment, you are just like many other people on a
long endless trip in my life. I am behind bars sitting
there, watching the passing parade, watching people
go by while I remain an outsider. That's what I think
treatment is—a passing parade of people" (Figure 16).

He then offered the next picture and said: "Basically treatment is a choice. I have all those eyes watching me. I am supposed to take this nice pure stuff
(referring to one pile) and avoid all this shitty messy
stuff, and I don't know which way to turn." I heard that
perhaps he was ready to grapple with the instinctual
dirty part of himself. I commented about the messy
part of himself and referred to all those people watching him. He laughed and said, "I guess there are an
awful lot of people watching me," to which I playfully
quipped, "That, indeed, makes you very important!"
(Figure 17).

In the next session he brought a big drawing
signed "grandiose" and laughed at himself, marking
the beginning of the expression of humor in his art

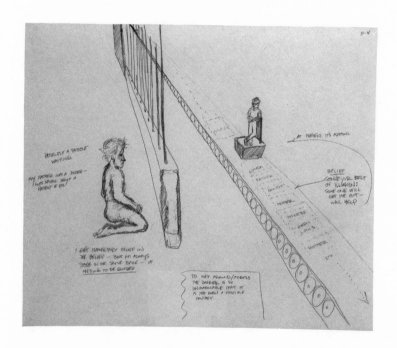

FIGURE 16

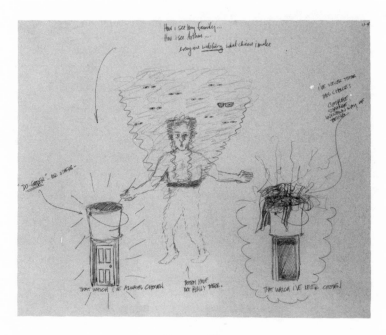

FIGURE 17

work. Our playful banter now seemed to counter-balance this man's heavy, gloomy tone. The final drawing described him and his family. He was carrying his family on his back (Figure 18). He described the sorrow, the weight, the oppression, and the feeling of time running out. His entire psychosomatic inner life seemed to be encapsulated in this picture. There was also an embryo encased in the back. I was forcefully struck with how the image and symbolism went far beyond the verbal metaphor in describing his pain, anger, and defensive approach to life. In one image he captured the burden of his family, his father, his mother, the problems with his energy, the feelings of passivity, and his inability to let go. The entire psychoaesthetic dimension of the transference was laid out before me.

I started to come down rather hard on George's use of masochistic suffering as a means of avoiding some of his own power. I interpreted his use of suffering as an attempt to maintain a cozy pain existence with his mother, until finally he shook with rage and fury. He was shocked by the sheer intensity of his rage, but was also rather pleased with himself. Rarely, if at all, had such a confrontation taken place with his own father. I literally felt that I was dragging him away from his embedded symbiosis with his mother. Here, through the vehicle of the real relationship, my own father imago was introduced as an important symbol of internalization.

The real relationship was balanced by a very active support of George's interest in the world of art. George and I met in the world of art where we shared our feelings about creativity, form, structure, and color. His pictures started taking on a vivid, open quality. He was

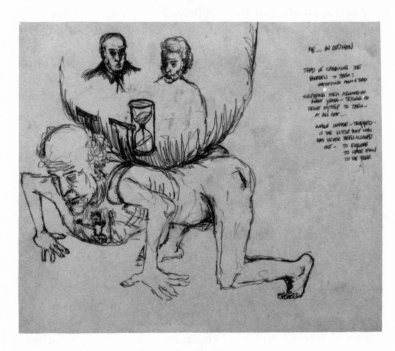

FIGURE 18

excited about this, and I shared some of his excitement. I wondered out loud what this development had to do with my son's interest in art. He pointed out to me that his interest in art was present long before I came on the scene. All these pictures were done in the privacy of his home. At this time, he also became more competitive toward me, but recognized that it was not safe to express these feelings. At a later point in treatment, with some trepidation he complained that he thought treatment was a failure and I, a washout. Much relieved that I didn't throw him out of my office, the pain in his back abated again.

Soon thereafter he started dealing with women and discovered that indeed not all were out to exploit or use him, nor did he have to be an appendage of them. Again, the supporting contact he received through the real relationship helped make it possible to face some of the deeper transferential issues regarding his connections to women.

Eventually, George left his job for work as an interior designer that was more consistent with his interests and aspirations as an artist. His back pain returned in full force, for he feared he would run out of money. As he cried like an enraged baby on the couch, I heard a screaming infant who feared desertion and wanted very much to be held. He described how hands were strapping his back like a vice. They were the masculine hands of his mother. Suddenly, these hands turned into braids and he visualized the intertwining of their mutual roots. Again, following this session, there was relief of the back pain.

In contrast to the first two presentations, George's schizoid predisposition was organized within a fairly delineated mental structure of self and object. Consequently, my emotional presence in the therapy was expressed quite differently than in the first two cases. His drawings were executed in his studio, for he required much less playful contact from me; yet the clear resonance of my interest in the creative process and the support of his artistic interest did make a difference in his ability to start investigating powerful male–female imagos. In the treatment, as part of the real relationship, the imparting of a male presence became an extremely important anchor to facilitate the processing of transference material. For one thing, I was actively present and provided a male with whom he could fight, argue, and make up. Through our dialogue, the pointed, clear, direct part of me made appropriate demands along with exhibiting support for his own interests and autonomy. Thus, our real relationship was characterized by a mixture of warmth along with a quality of feistiness. This was quite different from the real relationship with Joan, which required more gentleness, even though our discussions were spirited.

Each of the three case vignettes presents a particular coloration regarding the emotional tone and relatedness of patient and therapist. All the patients presented one common complaint: A feeling of isolation and aloneness, though their development had progressed differently creating different character defenses. With all three patients, the psychoaesthetics of the real relationship became an important organizer and anchor, permitting the unfolding of transference material. In Joan's case, the active interplay of a heated discussion between analyst and patient (or mother and child) regarding Zionism became a pivotal turning point in treatment. The interpretation of the transference along with active engagement promoted the emergence of the hidden self that dared to come out and risk the possibility of self-annihilation. In George's case, on the other hand, the projection of the analyst's male imago became an important facilitating backdrop to the working out of separation and individuation issues. Each step of individuation by the patient required reassurance that the analyst would not give up his supportive role. Most importantly, the experience of a male presence permitted the investigation of the symbiosis with the patient's mother. Finally, in the work with Doris, the therapeutic resonance of the early mother–child dyad became an important backdrop to investigate archaic superego systems and frightening internalizations. Here, the subtle holding and internalization of the real relationship became an extremely important factor in facilitating the opening up of a closed energy system that characterized the transference.

Thus, in all three cases, we can observe a resonance between analyst and patient facilitated by nonverbal images and visual, auditory, or kinesthetic modes of communication. Here, within a regenerative transitional space, energy communicated through nonverbal images became available for the processing of transference–countertransference material leading to new cognitive structures. Therapeutic acts by the analyst, along with verbal interpretations, became important pieces of structure in dealing with schizoid phenomena. In short, the active but controlled use of the real relationship, far from blunting the development of transference material, became a safe channel permitting new possibilities for the development of internal integrations. These issues are further elaborated on in the text, *Between Therapists: The Processing of Transference/Countertransference Material* (Robbins, 1988).

Implied in the above presentation are a number of possible directions for future research and theory building regarding the use of the real relationship in analytical treatment: (1) The nonverbal dimensions of closeness–distance, rhythm, tone, and "kinesthetic" field will be important determinants in the development and processing of transference material. (2) Empathic resonance with one's patients can be facilitated by an active use of important imagos drawn from the analyst's life history and utilized as a conduit for processing analytic material. (3) Therapeutic acts by the analyst may have important psychoaesthetic communicative value and may facilitate the processing of verbal interpretation.

7

Transitions and Transformations

The artist in the therapist accepts so-called accidents as a normal part of the creative process. Indeed, the unexpected and unplanned gives the art form energy and life, as a part of the artist's unconscious finds its way into aesthetic form and organization. I am often asked in introductory case seminars for my particular orientation and theoretical point of view regarding therapeutic practice. I answer with tongue-in-cheek: "I practice 'fuck-up therapy.' " The class usually responds with disbelief and amusement and requests further elaboration and clarification. I then share with them a basic axiom of treatment: Out of the so-called therapeutic errors comes the greatest possibility for patient progress. Of course, I qualify, there are distinct hazards and problems in making those therapeutic errors. Yet, as with any piece of art, accidents create the critical crises for the moment of transformation to take shape.

On reviewing the essence of this therapeutic attitude, I'm aware that I give up my preconceived notions or my therapeutic thought-out assumptions about any given patient. I feel out of control, yet I try to be present and regain my center. This indeed is no easy task for simultaneously I expose my frailties as a human being while at the same time I attempt to overcome my defensiveness and find my own therapeutic process. More often than not, the ensuing therapeutic dialogue has much to do with the patient's introject that has melted into my unconscious and now manifests itself through my disjunctive interventions. Yet I cannot run away from this therapeutic muddle that befalls both the patient and myself. Both patient and therapist are enclosed in darkness. To use another metaphor, we wallow in "therapeutic shitsville." The therapeutic induction has become charged and the treatment relationship feels like we are riding a wild bronco. Fantasy seems tightly enmeshed with reality as the transference illusion becomes larger than life. How often I have heard the refrain, "You are no longer like my parents, you *are* my parents." Yet in spite of the charged affects that permeate this dialogue, the nascent kernels of a separation process are evident; the patient now has a second chance to neutralize the intense affectivity associated with these introjects. The substance of this drama slowly forges a line between reality and illusion as the very heated words of this dialogue diminish the internal affects of dread and horror. The transference conflict has reached a state of crystallization. The patient no longer talks to an inner representation but to a real, live figure externalized in the treatment dialogue. Now the patient confronts, rages, despairs, and makes amends with his past, living in the embodiment of the therapist. The moment of transformation comes when the therapist finally becomes in charge of the emotional induction and redirects this energy as a healing and regenerative force in treatment. These induced affects, then, become the nexus of empathy and understanding in our patients' lives. All too often, this intense dialogue is prematurely cut off because both parties are frightened of entering into this black morass, since it can be crazy, confusing, and very disruptive. Yet, because of its very nature, there is enormous fluidity of boundaries for both participants, and as a consequence there is enormous possibility for change.

The patients whom I describe, of course, belong within the broad spectrum of primitive mental states. These patients communicate in a language that is often nonverbal and we respond to them in kind in spite of our many resolutions to the contrary. Their silent and penetrating pauses have unique emotional beats and amplifications. We sometimes observe a primitive and archaic dance that occurs between patient and therapist reverberating like the chant of a Greek chorus. We learn, in spite of all our knowledge, resolutions, and warnings, that therapeutic crises have a life of their own.

This space in which our heated therapeutic dialogue unfolds has both verbal and nonverbal parameters. We know that words cannot be separated from the therapeutic cadence and beat of treatment that I describe. We suspect that if we say too much, our responses become lost in the debris of defensiveness. Yet, by playing it safe and saying little, rage can encompass both parties and sink the therapeutic ship. When to speak and how much becomes a very delicate balance, and we learn to use all our senses like a finely tuned instrument.

Let me give a brief summary of the psychoaesthetic dialogue. The movement and music of treatment is woven like an interlacing composition. As therapists, we tune our sensitivity and become extremely alert to the patient's intonations, emotional resonance, and responsiveness as well as their bodily expressions, all accompanying or at one with the verbal communications. The nonverbal nuances, in particular, congeal into an image and organize this very complex structure of form, space, and time. In turn, these images become the core language of our senses and emotions that filters into the transitional space of treatment. Through these symbols and images, both therapeutic parties create two alternating processes that are in play with one another. On the one hand, the therapist mirrors the patient by joining and becoming part of the nonverbal substrata of contact. We move with our patient's words, resonate with their intonations, take on their emotional beat and rhythm so that an experience of oneness evolves. Through this process, the scars of separation and remorse are revisited.

There is much more that goes on in this emotional subterranean matrix. Our sensitivity to nonverbal communications requires an openness and a temporary loosening up of our own therapeutic boundaries. A state of oneness evolves even while we maintain our state of separateness. These transient identifications, however, cannot last indefinitely. We must find, as therapists, our own particular space and maintain our defined separateness and therapeutic role.

Here, then, lies the seeds for the disjunctive pain in treatment. We are open, responsive, and mirror the most subtle nonverbal interchanges that create a heightened form of intimacy. This intense form of relatedness is an essential part of treatment if we are to make contact on the deepest layers of our patient's existence. Fantasies, hopes, as well as dreams are fanned by this form of contact. Intermeshed with the intimacy, we define and shape the therapeutic transitional space with our interpretive efforts which create the *Sturm und Drang* of treatment. Defining and redefining the therapeutic structure, then, provides the balance for this gratifying interchange.

Thus, in spite of the fact that the therapeutic resonance offered to our patients is extremely relieving and pleasurable, we do not indulge our patient's hidden fantasies by becoming the good parent. There is a paradox, however, connected to our efforts in making contact, for we are offering a therapeutic form of love through intense relatedness.

Thus, the sensitive interplay of interpretive form against a background of therapeutic resonance becomes the nonverbal substance that facilitates the treatment relationship. Through this subtle exchange, an identification with the therapist slowly emerges providing a holding environment for our patients to transcend the pain of therapeutic separateness. The therapist, acting as a constant resonant structuring object, provides a fulcrum for the patient to organize insight material. Meaning, then, is found within the context of therapeutic nonverbal resonance. This subjective interplay of gratification and frustration becomes a primary aesthetic component of the treatment process.

A treatment session can be analogous to an artistic composition. Elements of the patient's story are reborn in treatment and woven into a unique fabric of space, time, and motion. Each element builds upon the other, creating a series of increasingly complex transitions. I am reminded of Shields' (Chapter 2) excellent analogy of musical composition and the structure of a therapy session. At times, this transitional space becomes deadened by an endless replay of the patient's story. The music stops, for there is no longer a building toward more complex themes. The therapist as well as the patient struggles to create a new order of transition that facilitates the building of complexity. Each transition leads to a greater sense of internal integration, as the parts come together with increasing depth and perspective. Periods of transformation are reached when the new elements leap over the bounds of history and find fresh meaning. We are then dealing not just with insight, but with an emotional–cognitive rendering of one's life.

The structure in which this process takes place is in the context of an increasing identification with the therapist who provides an anchor for a self to emerge within the patient. This self has struggled in treatment with deadness, repetitiousness, and disjunction and has gradually put together a new order out of a series of transitions and transformations in treatment.

I can think of a no more relevant diagnostic category than the borderline patient to illustrate these issues. The following represents one slice of a therapeutic interchange that occurred in session between a borderline patient and myself. My own images will be shared with the reader and will describe the nonverbal dance and music of treatment. In actuality, the patient lies fairly immobile on the couch.

Carol, a 39-year-old single woman, currently lives with her lover. We have worked together on a three-times-a-week basis for over three years. Her history reads like a prescription for an emotional disaster: Her mother, a self-involved, mocking, sadistic lady, externalized her self-hate onto her only daughter, my patient, and treated her like a nonhuman object. Frequently, the mother left the house and joined her husband in a local bar. The neighbors complained that her child was screaming and crying throughout the night. Later on, as she grew older, Carol ran away from home only to return defeated, or resorted to being destructive in the house by ruining furniture. Her mother's emotional sensitivity to her daughter seemed almost absent of care and relatedness. I recall a particular lament that still rings in my ears as I hear echoes of it in the transference relationship. "Don't leave me Mommy. Don't leave me Mommy." In her cry of childhood, she saw herself sitting on the bed in her mother's bedroom watching her primp for the night's activity. The mother laughed at her daughter, patted her on the head, and promised to return early. Both knew that this was a patent lie. The echo of my patient's cry goes on endlessly and she is full of tears and rage.

Her father was not much better: a depressed, withdrawn man, full of explosiveness, a chronic alcoholic, who was either assaultive or seductive to his daughter. The latter behavior was particularly apparent during

my patient's adolescent years when he used to invite
her to join him in bed. Here he fondled her while she
lay frozen; she later tried to avoid this encounter whenever possible. In later adolescence they fought, and on
one occasion she threw dishes at him. She recalls thinking to herself: "I've nothing to lose for they already hate
me." Fortunately, books gave her solace, for she with-
drew in her bedroom, barricaded from what was going
on in her family, and insulated from her feelings of
hopelessness and despair. Her peer relationships did
not provide much comfort or support, for she entered
the peer group feeling an endless cycle of inadequacy
and fear which stimulated very little positive regard
from her classmates. Literature offered her a connection to life, but also a safe retreat from reality. Books
also offered her soothing from the hard surface of her
family.

Currently Carol works as a high school social science teacher, feeling unqualified and inadequate in
meeting her students' needs. Her job demands an image of competency, something that feels very far away
from her grasp. She wonders whether she should leave
the field, but has no idea what else she could do. She
claims that her colleagues do not respect her and she is
convinced that they laugh at her behind her back. In
addition, her principal has assigned her to teach the
worst classes in the school. She has not been fired, however, and has been with her school for over five years.

During the course of treatment, I have observed
some ostensible gains. She is far more emotionally related and connected and does not ramble or blow up
with her friends or lover. Yet I wonder whether we have
accomplished enough even though I hear in the back-

ground faint echoes and accusations from the patient's past history. The patient often laments that there was good reason for her being such an object of hate. Somewhere, somehow it was her fault.

Without further elaboration, I will invite you, the reader, to our most recent emotional encounter in treatment. The time takes place after a long vacation break and the patient has difficulty returning to treatment. I have just received a call from her lover, Bob. I learn through him that Carol has become increasingly suicidal and Bob is worried about her safety. This comes on the heels of an enormous storm in treatment. In the previous session, I told Carol that if she cannot remain on the couch, she must leave. She shouted at me and claimed that she will never do this and stalked out of the room. This has happened before and, as in the past, I firmly held my ground. I implored her to remain on the couch but she refused to listen; she slammed the door and walked out. This has been the culmination of a long battle between us. Off the couch, I experience the patient as being swallowing and intrusive. She stares at me with open saucer eyes and I feel uncomfortable and unable to do my work under such a gaze. I therefore insist that she remain on the couch in spite of her protestations.

The stage is now set. I know our fight is but a smokescreen rising from her fear of being deserted and she needs a palpable demonstration of my interest and concern. Her fear has now turned into an insistent acting out to possess me. At times during the session we are both lost in the smoke, and I fear that I cannot extricate myself from my own defensiveness as we continue our exchange. The patient stalks and struts into the office, throwing her bag on the chair and lies down on the couch belligerently, with her hands folded. She looks ready for action. I brace myself for the storm and move back into my chair. I hear both hurt and anger in her voice, but detect her fear not far from the surface. She seems ready for a fight and I know she is far more comfortable combating me than dealing with the soft belly of her vulnerable feelings. There is a long silence and tension mounts. Neither one of us moves. Finally she speaks in a low throaty voice. She says that she does not know if she is merely living out her dependency with me. She suspects that she gets very little out of treatment. I have heard this chant before and I nod silently. She constantly plays it like a Greek chorus echoing in the background. "Should I be here in treatment?" "Maybe I should leave." At times I have directly challenged her. This has only produced more fear; yet, I wonder out loud if another therapist might be of more help. She is furious at me. "Don't say that," she spits back. I try now to backtrack. I become less stiff and loosen up my tight shoulders and neck and search for the round soft tones in me. I say, rather quietly, that it is very hard for her to feel warm and close while feeling dependent for she is furious at being impotent, as she feels that she has no rights in her state of dependency. She feels, in fact, that I call the shots. My hope in saying this is to offer a clear statement of her predicament. She readily agrees and visibly relaxes on the couch. I now hear her speak with a voice full of pain and anguish as well as accusation. "Why do you tell me to leave? Don't you know that's the last thing I want to hear from you? What kind of therapist are you?" Speaking with fury and hurt in her voice, her movements go in and out—first open and receptive, then backed away and constricted. I can imagine her looking soulful and angry and standing in the corner watching Mommy getting ready for the night's activity. I confess to her that I am indeed irritated and angry. Now, almost matching her melody, I move with round open tones and confess that my anger came out of my own feelings of impotency and frustration. Privately I have a quick vision of two lovers trying to make up to one another after a fight.

I continue my soft open movements and come closer to her. "I could understand how you feel very deserted since I have taken such a long vacation." "I don't believe what you're saying," she erupts. "You are happy to get rid of me. Frankly, I don't think you can stand me!" I matched the volley and mounting intensity with my voice, punctuating my statements clearly and forcefully: "Yes," I agree, "you can be obnoxious, and at times I cannot stand you, but that's not the main issue. I tell you to leave out of frustration." Again my words and movements are becoming sharp and angular. She would now have to decide, I said, whether I am a liar or telling the truth. She responds very quickly and relents: "You're not a liar. You tell the truth. But still in the background of my mind I think you hate me and want to get rid of me." The intensity in my voice goes up an octave or two and I stand firmly with my feet in the middle of the room and say clearly, "There are certain rules that we have to abide by. One is that you stay on the couch. Two, when you are feeling depressed or suicidal, I don't receive notes or messages from your lover. You must tell me directly; that is our agreement. You are not here to threaten or provoke me so I will come to your rescue. If you can't abide by those rules then I can't work with you." "You're just worried about your own skin," she screams at me. "You don't really care about me." I can see her arms flailing about ready to assault me. "That has nothing to do with it," I now say in a much softer, but equally intense voice. "The rule is simple—suicide is out! That's the agreement." She backs down and speaks in round imploring tones. "I didn't mean it anyway. I knew I wasn't going to do anything." I know that she is throwing me a bone, making a superficial attempt to make nice to me. I am cautious and wary and feel my eyebrows rise. I do not trust what she says. She then starts coming back and hisses, "I have to play by your rules. Take it or leave it. And there's no ifs, ands, or buts about it," she says. "That may be," I agree, and spoke again with a soft intense voice. "But those are the rules I need respected in order to treat you." She shouts at me, with raised fists, that I am a male chauvinist; that I am a boss and she doesn't like that—that I am just like her father. I do not want to get too involved with whether or not I am like her father and back away by simply stating, "I have the right to work the way I want to."

Carol switches the mood and she bounces away from me—and the intimacy. She cannot take the intensity of our exchange. I recognize that I have been speaking too much, moving too much, and she dances off into the corner of the room. She complains that she is furious at her lover. "Bob wonders whether I should see a new therapist. What right has he to tell me who I should see? I'm entitled to see whoever I want. He has no right to interfere with my treatment. I have not asked him for anything. What right has he got to com-

plain about my treatment? This is my private business."
She speaks with much agitation and anger and again I
could see her fists flailing as if not really connected to
her body. Another pause follows and then she states, "I
feel that you agree with him." I kick myself for not being silent but I want to engage her and so I move right
in and face up to her and state: "Why don't you ask me
directly?" "All right," she says. "I think you're annoyed
with me. I think you find me difficult." A long pause
follows. I softly said, "Yes, I find you difficult. But I
have always been clear as to why. Your self-beratements
and attacks are difficult to take and I sometimes feel
impotent in not knowing where to go or what to do. I
certainly do not want you to come here out of dependency if that is all you're getting out of treatment. If I
told you to leave, it was out of exasperation that you do
not follow the rules of treatment" (I feel my whole body
making a wide open sweep as to emphasize my convictions). The patient quickly replies with bitterness and
venom, "I can't understand that," she says accusingly. I
try to take distance by speaking rather softly, "But you
have not left." "Yes," she blurts out, "I am still here, but
God only knows why. You know, I came very close to
not being here." Again, I speak in a low, soft voice as
she goes higher in pitch. "But you are here." "I went
through a lot," she shouts out, "and if it was not for my
lover, I don't think I would have made it. He was as real
a reason as any for my being here. It was so painful,"
she laments as she bows her head and looks woefully at
the floor. She goes on, "I wasn't quite sure what I was
going to do. What would you have done," she said with
her voice trembling in rage, "if I didn't show up?"
Again, I speak softly and quietly, making soft, gentle,

forward movements, "I would have called you." She snapped back testily, "I don't believe you." Again, I speak slowly and with emphasis, "I would have called you." She replied now with more softness and placation, "I don't think you would lie to me. You try to be truthful. But something just keeps on telling me that I don't believe you—that I just can't believe. If I didn't show up," she says with a high-pitched challenge in her voice, "would you call me?" There is a sense of disbelief coming through in her high-pitched voice as she moves and jerks. Again, I repeat, "Yes, I would call you." I speak once more in a long, soft voice sweeping gently by her. I could envision my head being bowed and quiet. The patient sits back, "I don't know why you would. You told me I'm withholding." I move away from the patient and try to disengage from the invitation to combat. Then sidestepping, giving us more space, I say, "Is this what our disagreement is all about? If we have a problem," I emphasize, "we can work it out." The patient shoots back like a spitfire, "I don't feel like that." I quickly retorted, "That's your greatest fear." I hear in my voice an accusation; once again we are in combat. I realize it as soon as I say it, but I can't stop myself. I feel on the defensive, and I find it difficult to regain my center, to understand and feel what is happening so I move ahead ineffectively. "You don't want me to tell you to go away. But you seem to dare it, provoke it, and in fact challenge it. It seems as if we are living out your fear. You always seem to be daring it to happen." The patient, now angered, replies, "I don't believe your concern and I don't understand it."

I know, in retrospect, that we are out of sync with one another and we are now dancing in two different spaces; she on one side of the room, myself on the other. We move, not seeing or hearing one another. I try to regain my balance and to refocus myself on the patient's space. I try to go beneath my defensiveness and understand my quiet over our mutual separateness. Slowly I start listening to my body and say, "If I told you you weren't unlovable and that you were valuable would you believe me?" A long pause follows. The patient stops in her tracks. I seem to have gotten her attention. I should be satisfied with this, but I cannot stop myself; I am still responding to my internal anxiety. I am too identified with her pain of separateness and as a result not in charge of my process. I hear myself speaking high in my throat. "You believe something else even though intellectually you understand what I'm talking about. That's where you bring your family into this office. It just doesn't go anywhere." And after a long pause, I commented, "I simply don't know exactly what to do." I hear frustration, pain, and a plea in my voice. Now there is much silence. The patient replies with equal pain, "I don't know what to do either." Finally, we are moving with one another. Looking pained, moving slowly and quietly, with intense thick movements I join her by saying: "I am a far cry from your parents. I do not dispose of you." The patient pushes back, "You are not a far cry from my parents. You are as explosive as my father. You hurt me." I then almost sink down and reply: "Yes, I am." I went on. "You believe that I am your family. How can I help you understand the difference between the transference and reality?" The patient now speaks with a much softer and slower cadence and becomes more thoughtful and reflective. She replies, "I don't understand myself." I mirror her question in the tone of my voice: "Perhaps life doesn't have to end up the way it was in childhood." The patient amplifies her predicament. "When I was growing up it was not just from my parents; it was from the other kids too." "Yes," I echo, with the same tone and resonance, "one thing led to another." And then I reply, hearing a faint hollowness in my voice, "It's time to see if we can separate from the past." The patient responds with somewhat higher vocal intensity, daring me to look at her, with open saucer eyes and directness. "I'm not an easy person to live with." "All that," I say in measured soft tones, "may be true. But whatever our problems are, we can work them out. I do not wish to get rid of you." I then, once again, lose my center. I become too talky. I cannot allow the intensity of the moment to sink in. My voice becomes higher and I move with my head disengaged from my center. "You are trying to make the past come alive here in our relationship and we must look at it." The patient replies with anguish, "I just don't know what to do with that." And I quickly replied, "I would never let you walk out." The patient now lashes back. "You know damn well," she says with exclamation and raised fist, "I couldn't walk out. I would if I could." I reply quickly, "Look, patients and therapists have difficulties in treatment. That's part of treatment, but this is something we can talk about. Termination is always a mutual process." "I don't know that," she shoots back. "All I hear is you want to get rid of me." "I have a problem," I said, "in making my rules clear without it sounding like a threat." I now begin to feel more centered and open. "I am sorry that disturbs you, but," I add, "you cannot play with suicide, even as a threat." She now backtracks, and with her hands outraised, says, "I was angry. I wasn't really going to do anything." "Then let us get down to the real issues," I said, matching her directness. "The real issues are not the couch or the chair, but the fact that the vacation has been a long and difficult one for you to bear. You were starting to feel warm and close to me in June and then I left. You felt deserted and then we got embroiled in an awfully big fight." A long pause follows and the patient replies very softly, "I'm sorry about my transference." I quickly retort, "There are no apologies needed. Let's take some distance and look at it. Let's not get lost in another fight. Can we just look at how scared you are when you feel dependent?" She is more open and reflective and agrees that she's furious about her dependency—that she feels she has to accept anything from me. "I don't want," I say slowly, "for you to be a victim of your dependency." The patient now laments, with tears in her voice, "I felt close to you in June. Things were going pretty well. You were treating me fairly. And then everything seemed to change, as if whatever good that came out of the treatment never took hold. I just felt as bad as I always did. I am furious at you." I agree that I can see how she could be furious at me. "Yes," she says, "and I will never forgive you for that." The patient continues to talk with much vehemence and anger. "Your leaving was just kind of leaving me to fend for myself." I readily agree that I could see her point of view. "It was like," she says, "like you were pulling the rug right out from under me. What I get from you," she says, "is that your need to take care of yourself by going away is so damn important that you don't give a rap about me in the least." The patient speaks with conviction. Her movements are clean, straight, and very centered. I respond with equally direct, clear movements. I say, "That is so, that I was very involved in my own need to take a vacation; that was important to me, but then you felt like just another patient. It brings up the reality that I cannot fill up that big space inside of you and you hate me for it." "What do you mean?" she says, starting to looking hurt and chagrined, moving back cautiously. "That you can't stand the business aspect of treatment." "I pay my fees," she says. I commented that, "Often I hear you say you want to be special. That you don't want to be just another face in a long parade of patients. And because you are not special, often I hear you saying you are a nobody." "I am a nobody," she shoots back. "That," I calmly retort, "is something you bring from your past. Coming here as a patient doesn't make you a nobody. That's a feeling you have and it's not a fact."

We seem to be twisting in and out with one another, yet remain related. The patient returns to the topic of the couch. I can envision her with her hands on her hips pacing up and down the room. "Why can't I sit up? Sometimes I need to see you. I think you are overly rigid and you don't understand what I need. Frankly, there are plenty of therapists who allow their patients to sit up. I can't understand you; you seem so flexible in so many other things and here you act like a stupid, classical, asinine therapist." My pace became very slow, balancing her rapid fire movements. "Perhaps," I said, "following this rule may be a way of showing some type of mutual respect between us." "If I always have to follow your rule," she spits out with a power thrust, "I feel I will have to leave. If you don't trust that I know what I need, what's the point of going on?" I continue my slow, deliberate pace, "That just makes you feel like a patient and that's what's infuriating you. It's like a wound that just sticks right inside of you." I could imagine her running up and standing over me. "Sometimes I don't give a rap about your rules. I don't feel I have to listen to you all the time," said with protest and anger. I move even more slowly. "Perhaps you don't have to listen to me," I said, "but one rule you have to follow and that is you have to stay on that couch. This upsets you." The patient is now on the verge of tears, and says, "I just don't know how to look at all this. It makes me feel so bad. I feel so confused. I just don't understand how to deal with this transference that you keep on referring to." I now met her with equal softness and replied, "When you were younger there was nobody there to listen to your feelings. That is something we can do here. All these feelings that you experience from the past, feeling alone and deserted, we can talk about them. I can be here and listen." She now seems apologetic, but, in spite of herself shoots back, "I don't want to accept the fact that I'm nobody. If that's what accepting reality is, then I don't want it." I bounce back, "That's part of the transference." She then retreated to a thoughtful position, her head slightly bowed, looking inward. "How can I be somebody when I can't get respect from anybody?" "Maybe," I say, "the first thing we have to do is at least respect what we are doing here. I understand that just being able to survive was important but maybe we have to look at the meaning of what this is all about." And now I added with a gentle sweep of my hand, "Sometimes I don't think you give a damn about meaning." The patient protests in a loud voice, and starts to prance back and forth. "That's not true. I do care, but I just don't know what to do about it." I then respond with directness, "I'm asking you to reflect and think about it." The patient now becomes plaintive. "I hear that. I try to think but it hasn't changed anything." I imagine the patient standing up and looking over me with raised voice and arms on her hips. "This is not transference. You want to get rid of me. That's based on last week's experience. I'm supposed to behave irrationally, and if I behave irrationally, I get punished." I continue in slow, measured tones even though I feel she is standing over me. "We go from the irrational to the rational back and forth and that's how we talk about our feelings here in treatment." The patient seems to be soothed by this and sits and starts to reflect inward. "Maybe I'm not capable of doing this," with pointed emphasis. I challenge that. "You are quite capable." "How do you know?" she says, now seeming to walk furiously up and down the room. "Anyone is," I reply in slow, measured tones. "You know," she says, openly looking for succor, "I was pretty crazy this weekend. I don't think you realize that." In my mind I see her arms raised, her face open, and yet she speaks with a most painful affect. "I wanted to kill you or myself in a very real way, and that's crazy." I say, "You described it very well and I understand what you're talking about." She then interrupts me. "If it wasn't for my lover I don't know what I would have done. I felt betrayed by you." There is accusation in her voice—hurt, anguish—and then we sit through one of the longest in our intense dialogue. The room is very quiet.

The patient then continues. "I don't know if I can do what you're asking me to do. I don't know," she emphasized with a question in her voice. "I don't know what it is to be patient. I don't know what it is to get distance. I understand the words that you're saying, but I just can't make sense out of it." I then slowly but firmly reply, "Something very important happened here. You shared painful feelings with me. They are similar to those you felt with your family. If your family ever heard these feelings they wouldn't have the foggiest idea what you're talking about. But I have listened, we've talked back and forth, we've argued, we've shared a lot, and that's something that never went on in your family." "You know," she says, seemingly more reflective and passive, "With all your apologies and explanations, I don't think they make one bit of difference." "Yes," I say, "that's true. They don't make a difference. I can never make up for the pain of this week, nor can I make up for the pain of your whole childhood and past." In saying these words, I now feel more present and centered, and the patient likewise seems to be more present than ever before. Both of us, standing very firmly on the ground, looking at each other straight in the eye, speaking as honestly as we could, then pause quietly for a long time.

I break the silence with, "And that's the biggest pill for you to swallow." The patient agrees and the silence of meaning envelops both of us. She then starts to speak in soft tones. "Under no circumstances could I tolerate being discarded. I know that you're quite capable of doing it. How do I know that you won't say to me, 'Go see another therapist?'" I know that it is difficult for us to be so centered, and I try to listen and respond with care. "Termination is a mutual process." I echo this over and over again. The patient retorts, both with anguish and plea, "I don't want you to be in a position of terminating me or wanting to terminate me and my not wanting it." Again, there is a hushed silence in the room. "We have rights, however," I then speak slowly, "to talk about our differences in treatment. It does not mean that I cannot confront you about certain issues that come up between us." In my mind, I envision the patient about to get off the couch and again run up and down the room. "You just told me," she says, with vehemence in her voice, "that things are not being productive." I reply very quickly, "This has been one of the most productive periods of our entire relationship." She sniped back, "But I still am not cooperating. I still disagree with you. I don't think that I am being cooperative at all." Then she says with enormous emphasis, force, and timber in her voice, "You can't make me into a rag doll." I am surprised and explain, "I would never want you to be a rag doll. I could never take your soul away. You were left with your rag doll as a child. Your rag doll is yours. But you are not going to become one and I don't want you to be one." "But you want me to be a rag doll," she protested. "You haven't been acting like one today," I offer. I then try to justify my behavior and begin speaking too fast. My voice is locked up in my throat. "Perhaps I've been insistent today about the transference. That comes out of my anxiety about helping you. I know you don't want to be treated like a thing." The patient now protests, "I'm not very smart, I have trouble. I guess," she says reluctantly, "you are right. I don't know how to get distance and understand this." I reply with an equally soothing voice, "The intensity of your feelings is very overwhelming." A long pause follows and then she moves in a direction that seems both conciliatory and open, "Maybe I do believe you. I don't know." She continues, "Just give me time." And then, after another pause, she complains, "I am still," almost as a way of trying to justify her behavior, "I am still not sleeping at night. I stay up watching TV. Nothing seems to help. I don't want to do this. Then I am ruined for work. I just can't sleep." She then shifts into another realm of consciousness. She looks like she is becoming more reflective. "I have a dream to tell you. My lover and I were in a boat. We seemed to be put into the bottom of the ship, in a hole with all the freight and baggage. We saw a light coming from the top. There wasn't a lot of air coming through and we could hardly breathe. I don't understand why we were there. I wanted to get out. Neither of us could find a way out, and we felt trapped." I ask her if she has any thoughts about the dream; then she says, "I don't really remember the dream. I don't have much to say about it." Both of us are trying to get out of a dark hole and I add, "I believe you see some light coming through the darkness. Perhaps that is some of the light that you may find here in treatment." She appears to ignore my comments and goes back to her lover. "I was very angry at Bob, for even though he was very helpful this weekend, he kept on annoying me as well, wondering if I was really being helped by you. I know I gave him plenty to worry about, feeling so depressed, but he's very insensitive to me. He had no right to raise the possibility of my seeing someone else. That's none of his business. He wasn't sensitive to what I needed, and I think sometimes you are as insensitive as he is. I really don't know how you feel about me. I know you're very supportive and helpful in my work just like Bob is. He wants to help and so do you. But deep inside I'm not really sure whether either of you really cares." We are nearing the end of the session and I conclude by saying that at least we are in the dark hole together, stuck with all the baggage and freight. I also think to myself, we are on a ship, we are moving, and even though we are encased in blackness, there is light coming down into that deep hole.

As I now review the session I am aware of the irreconcilable forces of reality and illusion, constantly battling one another. I seemed to be swept up into a Greek tragedy where the inevitable forces of fate took on their own momentum in spite of my efforts to make a change in our therapeutic direction. My associations to this session led immediately to a play I saw a few years ago entitled "Women of Troy." As I recall, it was an avant-garde play in which the audience became part of the theatrical event. We were participants and audience, watching Helen being led to the sacrificial altar. She hissed and screamed; she was enraged, yet she had dignity, for she felt like a sacrificial lamb and took vengeance on all the people who hated her. The mob turned on her and wanted her blood. I see my patient as this sacrificial lamb of her family who is being punished for forbidden love. With terror she is approaching the forbidden love of her father and I suspect that she expects the gods to come down and destroy her. I am also equally aware of my vulnerability in the session. I see myself preaching and lecturing—the telltale signs that I am becoming very anxious and defensive. Her pain and anguish cuts into a deep core of me; I often lose my separateness and participate as part of the mob scene. At times I regain my center and recognize that I am less than perfect. Hopefully, I have set the stage that someday Carol will forgive me for not making up for the sins and lack of her parents. I feel her fury and anger which borders on murderousness. Yet something is different in the session. At times we seem to deeply understand each other. "Give me time," she says. "Let me have some time so I can digest this." We both recognize that working out the transference is something that cannot be proselytized or taught but must be processed. Hopefully she has felt a piece of the reality while speaking to her introjects of the past. Perhaps out of this dialogue a real separation of past and present can be enacted.

The end of our session was marked by emotional intensity, fear, hurt, accusation, fury, and pain, yet was coupled with significant moments of pause and reflection. The disjointed acting out, where both therapeutic parties were not in charge of their bodies, was replaced by moments of reflection. These moments had elements of transcendence and transformation. Here there is hope that something new can happen in spite of loss and deprivation, and in spite of her fear and vulnerability. I made no apologies for my defensiveness, rambling, or preaching. Her pain seemed to resonate with a very deep hole that lies inside of me. Slowly I attempted to regain my presence as a therapist and give structure and clarity as well as form to the reality of our relationship. At times we also mirrored, moved, and danced with one another, in pain, anguish, and at moments, in peace. And so, the session ended, only to be continued on the next day.

Now, months later, upon reviewing this session, I blanch with embarrassment as I witness such obvious breaks in analytic decorum. Most importantly, I "acted out" some of my patient's worst fears regarding a therapeutic relationship. I threatened her with abandonment if she could not abide by my rules. I was irritated and often angry, as well as defensive and pompous, and furthered her sense of smallness. At times I was "all over her" and she could not breathe, and gave ample testimony to this emotional state in her dream. The pain of not being everything for Carol was too much for me, and I was equally wounded and hurt. My struggle to find my own separateness was all too patently clear. In short, I was at times empathically out of sync with my patient, feeling frequently out of control and off center.

In spite of these problems and my point is perhaps because of them, both of us were drawn to face up to our mutual limitations and shortcomings as human beings. We were engaged in a process parallel to the process of artistic composition. We danced and sang together, sometimes in mutual resonance, often in polarized contrasts. On other occasions, we moved in a spiral, weaving in and out. The form of our interchange paralleled the meaning of the content. When the process was most creatively engaged, we were separate yet together—together in that we were merged into a dialogue, at times to the point where I allowed her introjects to infect my behavior, and separate in that we evolved a balance and transitional rhythm back and forth, from the energy of our affects that opened possibilities to transform stale content and pattern in the present creative momentum of the session. We played with form and space and time as well as motion in our building of a thematic statement. The intonations of our voices, the pitch, intensity, and rhythm built a structure of communication that evolved out of a vortex of many interfacing levels. And then, too, the process abruptly stopped. The diptych of the communication process split and fragmented into separate spaces. The therapeutic field of communication could not contain the sheer intensity of affects and we danced and sang alone waiting to find new doorways for entry into the therapeutic process.

This therapeutic composition, then, built with verbal and nonverbal structures, moved into a series of transitions. With short bursts of contact, the theme of dependency, abandonment, rage, and impotency played itself out, sometimes covered by secondary skirmishes around the couch, but moved both sharply and painfully into the arena of abandonment and impotency over my vacation. Questions and declarations followed: Do I have rights if I am so dependent? Does love mean possession? Indeed, does love create fusion? These transitions interlocked with one another through the smoke and fire of our engagement.

My therapeutic errors must be faced with a degree of openness and nondefensiveness that demands all the discipline I can muster. Here, in this space, lies the seeds for a therapeutic transformational process. Stripped of my protective role of therapist, I view our frailties as human beings. Both of us finally arrive in "shitsville"; we are both impotent and beside ourselves. Yet, in our mutual despair, we are joined in that black spot of existence, for there are no boundaries, but a very primitive connection; at rockbottom, despair. In this black space, the possibilities for new forms arise; for both of us now experience contact beyond our protective self-imposed walls of alienation. The possibilities for change, then, occur when we move past the individual boundaries of our existence and free the energy of the self to seek new forms of containment.

Thus, together we mirror moments of utter despair and impotency. The therapeutic theme takes on a new order. Both participants realize that treatment cannot remove the hurt and loss of abandonment. In that realization, however, there is hope, for in contrast to the past we can talk, process, and recognize our mutual deficiencies. In this dialogue lies the possibility for healing. Both of us face this piece of therapeutic truth and in the realization we find permission to be separate but together.

Through this therapeutic composition, the transition phase makes a symbolic leap. The patient's dream offers a new order to our dialogue. The black hole has light streaming into it, yet we are suffocating in our black space. We are together in that black hole, and the ship is moving. The drama of therapy now appears larger than life as it creates and develops a theme of blackness leading into light. Herein lies the hope of treatment: That a new order can be created out of the chaos and despair of our past existence.

Personal therapy for the therapist can never completely control the leakage and spillage over of the therapist's unconscious. At best, our treatment will offer us the tools to extricate ourselves from the mess of the transference–countertransference bind rather than sinking into it further. Likewise, treatment cannot always be reduced to transference and counter-transference phenomena. The next chapter leads to a natural development of a psychoaesthetic perspective: The therapist as a container of color, space, form, and light, and as a symbol of hope and healing.

8

Energy, Light, Color, and Space
Interfaces with an Object
Relations Approach to Therapy

An analogy can be drawn between rereading a published article or revisiting a personal work of art that was completed a number of years ago and an old love affair. Like an old love affair, one feels strangely detached and removed. From this distance, I find myself reflecting on what all the pain and intensity was about. Now, in fact, I observe the flaws and problems of a published article or work of art that escaped my scrutiny before because I was so close to the experience. This observation applies to an article entitled "Interpretation as a Means of Organizing Psychological Space within the Transference/Countertransference Relationship" (Robbins, 1984), which I presented at a national conference on the use of interpretation in psychoanalytic practice.

Much of what I stated still remains relevant. More importantly, the missing parts bear special noting. Why, I ask myself, did I present a clinical example that did not illustrate the introjective process or relevant developmental issues that highlight an object-relations approach to treatment? This was my assigned task in the conference, to offer such a presentation. Chapter 5 may offer some clues on this matter since in retrospect I now see that unconsciously I was already working on the issue of transcendence and transformation.

The patient discussed in Chapter 5, a deprived and depressed woman, lives out her life experiencing no exit from her state of hopelessness and sameness. During therapy sessions, her black, hollow spot would ominously envelop the office. I attempted, through my interpretive efforts, to embody her with power and impact. Now, after further review, I discern a new dimension to my containment of her unending blackness. I realize that I have become a container for the patient's feelings of hope and luminosity. I now recognize that this patient was too frightened to hope that her life could change and required the therapist to transform her dreaded sense of despair into an image of light and luminosity. Hope and transcendence are frightening affects for any patient to bear, particularly for those who are ensconced in blackness and depression. Yet all of us possess the capacity for transcendence and hope, but these affects may create enormous threats to one's past connections and associations about the world we live in. In short, it is better to be linked to these frightening beliefs than to separate and face the panic of aloneness. The following represents the original article that I presented at the National Conference on the Use of Interpretation in Psychoanalytic Practice.

In preparing this talk on the use of interpretation, a memory intruded into my consciousness which I'd like to share with you. I remember vividly making my first speech, at my confirmation. I recall all my 13-year-old's discomfort as I stood at the pulpit with my legs quaking and my voice rather tense. Then I spotted my mother in the audience. There she was, looking down with her hand on her head, and I knew she was thinking, "Oh, is he going to make a fool of me today?"

I responded to this challenge with some arrogance and a degree or provocation. I was torn by fear of having to prove myself and not wanting to have to assert my worth.

The relationship of my internal representations of the arrogant, frightened boy and his mother often has made itself felt in the psychological space between myself and others. This dyad projected outward acquired its own energy, intensity, sensibility, and coloration, as well as volume and rhythm. I still see at times in my professional interactions with patients, students, and audiences the presence of that child as I again become somewhat arrogant, provocative, and frightened. Perhaps you can detect a bit of that today as I look out at you all in the audience and think how very mature and grown-up you look!

I brought this type of relationship to my analyst almost from the very first day of treatment, as I said to him rather provocatively: "I'm entering analytic training and I think I should withdraw. I don't believe I have the stuff to be an analyst. I frankly think I should be in marketing research. That's something I can hold onto that's clear, specific, statistical, and can make me money."

I confessed readily that I wasn't quite sure whether I could make a living as an analyst. The frightened, arrogant boy within me nagged that it was such a grown-up world: Who would want to see *me*?

My analyst's response was surprising. He replied that he saw no reason why I couldn't be an analyst. Very strange, indeed. Here I thought an analyst was supposed to be neutral and to analyze my defenses, yet he was encouraging me. I walked out of that session feeling a tremendous sense of relief.

At a much later date, I acquired a more cognitive sense of this interaction. His response was quite clearly an interpretive intervention designed to differentiate the past relationship, regenerated in the transference, from the real present. His manner, attitude, and presence supported rather than undermined the little boy who was both trying to prove himself and wanting to withdraw from it all.

Interpretation, as I utilize it in my clinical practice, directly reflects my theoretical roots, which are in object relations theory. Within this context, I, as a therapist, work first to build integration and cohesiveness in a patient's sense of "self" that suffers from deficits in early nurturing and then to promote separation and individuation. Interpretations, then, spring from a strong sense of where the client is developmentally, transferentially, and emotionally, and they involve an organizing response on my part on both verbal and nonverbal levels. My goal is to take the germ of an awareness floating between us and to mold it into a communication that makes the intangible explicit. In working this way, I move between primary and secondary processes, using image, metaphor, and linear description. I remain open but controlled; spontaneous but not wild. Clearly, interpretation in this sense involves more than making the unconscious conscious or connecting past and present. It gives shape and form to the myriad relationships being played out in the psychological space between therapist and patient as their internalized objects make contact and react to one another.

To give you a better sense of what this actually looks like, I'd like to invite you into my office to meet a 25-year-old woman who has been in analysis for 5 years. As in most of our sessions, she barely looks at me as she moves to the couch with her face tight and drawn. Her averted gaze seems to cry out, "Don't look at me, I'm in too much pain and feel too vulnerable."

There's an explosive quality to the way she laments about first one person in her life, then another. She complains of her husband: "Why can't he listen to me; he seems too preoccupied with himself," then turns her attention to her sister, who makes her feel angry and unwanted. "Can't she ever pick up the phone and speak to me? Of course, she doesn't want anything to do with me!" Again the focus shifts, this time to herself as she proclaims, "I can't stand to hear my voice. How can *anyone* listen to me?" The fury, pain, and bitterness that tellingly betray how unlovable she feels are reflected in the rigidity and tautness of her whole body. She looks as though she could explode.

Her associations take another turn and she remembers when she was 10 years old. She recalls walking on stage as an extra in a local opera company, and says, nostalgically, "What fun it was to dress up in costume, to be on stage, to play in the world of make believe!"

She doesn't know why she thinks of this, and goes back to complaining about her husband: "Why doesn't he listen to me? Yet why should anyone listen to me?"

Now I receive her attention and she says: "You must be very bored hearing this over and over again. I know I'm tiresome, and you are probably just waiting for the session to be over."

As I consider how best to respond to this tirade, I recall that my past attempts to be empathic have not always been successful. Although this patient has come to feel better about herself, she still is overcome by waves of self-derision. As much as the hurt child in her wants desperately to be held and touched, her intense bond with the unloving mother of her past undermines her ability to let the craving for closeness be satisfied in the present. As though she is reading my mind she cries out: "I don't trust your attempts to be caring. They're phony. I don't matter, you're just doing a job."

I can almost see her mother standing between us, denying my patient's existence. Bored and preoccupied with herself, this mother plants the seeds in her child of negligible self-worth as the baby's impotent screams go unanswered. It is the specter of this mother that has cut off my attempts at empathy.

Reinforcing this, however, is a father who basically feels contempt for women. As his presence permeates the room, I can hear him grumbling to my patient to get married and have children. "Forget a career," he says, "that's for men."

My patient's fury and envy of men screams out at me as she spits: "You have it all, Robbins: A practice, reputation, money. You can afford to be tolerant of me, but I know I'm really just like all the other patients, and I doubt if you ever think of me once the session's over."

Rather than answering immediately, I decide to let the atmosphere in the room invade my being. Something entirely new enters my consciousness. A graphic image emerges: Powerful red and black rays, vibrating with energy, fill my awareness as they radiate from the core of my patient. Reminiscent of a psychedelic experience, intense and vivid colors bleed into one another and shoot in all directions. Deep inside the body of this image I see a small pink ray.

With this picture, a new understanding of my patient strikes me. In the past, I've had little trouble being sensitive to her impotence and feelings of neglect, but the sheer intensity and force of this woman's internal world had been lost in the process.

I decide to share this image with my patient after considering the possibility that I may be acting out a countertransference seduction. My concern is that my difficulty in tolerating the strong sense of aloneness and futility this patient induces in me is provoking a desperate attempt to connect via the sharing of my image. The profundity of my patient's reaction, however, confirms the appropriateness of my decision. For the first time, all sound ceases and the remainder of the session is filled with a gentle, meditative silence. There has been some transformation in how my patient sees and experiences herself that is visible in the quiet way she walks out of the office.

When I see her again, it takes some time for her to get back to the previous session, but she finally tells me that she has felt peculiar. "I couldn't believe what was happening to me," she says. "I've often thought of myself as having so much in me, and yet I've heard people like myself described as being empty. I know I'm not empty, and your description touched and moved me. I don't quite understand it. I know that I created this response in you, but I still find it hard to believe—it's so very full..."

In this brief encounter, we can observe the subtle merger of psychodynamics and aesthetic principles of form and energy shaping psychological space into a new dimension. My patient and I had done endless work on penis envy, castration anxiety, resistances, hostility, and dependency, but interpretations of this nature, though accurate enough, merely served to accentuate and reinforce my patient's sense of powerlessness.

In this episode, a shift occurred in figure and ground. The patient's sense of strength, power, and worth was affirmed. The impotent, castrated girl discovered power, while the father/therapist responded and was affected by the strength and intensity of her pain, rage, and despair. The patient felt in charge of her life, and for a moment, could move the unmovable. She needed this experience of having the energy and force that come from a sense of self-worth and power before she could have the strength to look at underlying issues and make further connections. Here, image and words, mediated by a merger of primary and secondary processes, form a continuous frame of subjective and objective reality that reflects the transference–countertransference relationship and the psychological space between patient and therapist.

Implicit in these ideas is the notion that relationships are characterized by different energy systems that shape and form the space around us. Within each system, there are different degrees of openness or closure, completeness or incompleteness. In terms of primitive mental states, the psychoanalyst offers a piece of himself or herself to help move the energy system from one level of differentiation to another.

I'd like to spend a moment to clarify what I mean by the term "psychological space." This "space," as I see it, is the product of complex interactions of objective and subjective levels that occur the moment a patient and therapist begin to work together. Past and present merge to create a mood and atmosphere unique to a particular dyad. The inner representations of past relationships are the stuff of this interaction, as they speak of the "me" and "you" within each person that create individual perceptions of the world and consequently also shape the surrounding social world's response to the individual. Multiple levels of consciousness are at work.

Art psychoanalysis, then, offers the possibility for psychological space, or that which is created through the interactions of two individuals, to be reorganized by mirroring or complementarity (offering opposites). This space has much in common with what Winnicott (1971) calls transitional space. It is an intermediate area that is neither inside nor outside, but makes a bridge between subjective and objective reality. By extension, dead or "pathological space" can also be created in the relationship when expression is weighed down by oppressive defenses. Here, relationships are experienced and programmed to recreate sterile childhood interactions.

In order to recreate the transitional space so necessary to bridge inner and outer realities, both patient and therapist must be prepared to play. In fact,

Winnicott describes treatment as play, or in some cases, as helping the patient to move toward being able to play. If psychoanalysts are to serve this role, they likewise must be ready to play. Play, as described by Winnicott, is not aimless activity or simply having fun, although fun may be one of the ingredients. The essence of play in therapy involves the capacity to lose intellectual controls and to become non-goal-oriented and open-ended in experiencing and working with the psychological space of patients. Here, images and symbols move into consciousness with their own logic and organization regarding time and place. In symbolic play, form and content become one through a synthesis of primary and secondary processes, also allowing the merging of bound and unbound energy and a balancing between fusion and separateness, organization, and loss of control.

Therapeutic play thus becomes a means by which we create a holding environment of resonance and relatedness with our patients. Like a child and mother, each type of resonance has its own aesthetic form: some being very gentle, some containing much space, some demanding close holding. Within each holding pattern, we, as analysts, find the appropriate rhythm of our child/patient to create the space and a subtle balance between our energy and that of our patient.

The challenge for the psychoanalyst is to provide an experience that keeps therapeutic space alive. What is called upon is the psychoanalyst's artistry in using his or her conscious symbolic awareness of the patient's communications along with play to keep the therapeutic process moving.

Likewise, each patient–analyst dyad creates its own use of artistry. For instance, with some patients I find myself receding into the background as they seemingly fill the room with bright colors and energy. Here, I become the container for their communications. With other patients, whose presences are so faint and tenuous that I can barely see them, I try to reverse the flow of energy in the attempt to organize and solidify the vague nuances floating about us. In all cases, the dimensions between analyst and patient have their own particular volume, rhythm, and energy, as well as a continuum of distance and closeness. Words are used to structure the energy and images generated.

Potentially, either participant can become the organizer or artist, shaping and mirroring the essence of the other. In the best of circumstances, the analyst is both one with his patient and separate, organizing primary- and secondary-process communications into a broadened statement of meaning and self-cohesion. Although this is likewise true for the patient, it is presumed that the analyst's mastery and control of this process will be somewhat ahead of the patient's. In the clinical example I gave, my inability to allow primary-process material to enter conscious awareness was masked by detached empathic relatedness. Perhaps there was also an arrogant little boy needing to prove himself. Ironically, the patient's sheer force and intensity most likely enhanced this.

The concepts of artist and artistry used in describing this interaction bring to mind the analogy of a diptych painting. Two art objects are separate yet interconnected, each enhancing the other, giving

strength and power to one another, while still maintaining separateness. In the analytic interchange of my example, my response recognizes the patient's power as
well as her soft, vulnerable part, giving new organization to our mutual awareness of one another. Here, each
of us gives something different in psychic essence to
the other. By contrast, my past interventions and reflections of her pain and despair augmented feelings of impotence. In these instances, neither of our pictures
added to the other. At least, impotence and pain are
transformed into power; softness and vulnerability are
surrounded by force and direction. I, in turn, am awed
by her intensity and strength.

Within this context, interpretation becomes a dynamic intervention in which the therapist utilizes himself completely. Parallels with my experience as a
sculptor come to mind. Here, I sometimes find myself
on what feels like an endless plateau. At times I turn
my stone upside down so I can acquire a new perspective. In other instances, I walk away from my work and
give myself a break. In general, I keep my perceptions
open and try to avoid premature closure or facile solutions to the problems. There is much hard work and an
enormous amount of trial and error involved. So it is,
too, with patients. As in a fine work of art, an interpretation that truly opens up new areas of the self is
infrequent and is preceded by much preparation.

A great deal of this preparation has to do with the
sensitive balancing of space, energy, and opposites of
all sorts. Also involved in this process is a familiarity
with the psychic territory so that we can move with
comfort. Each patient and therapist grapples, one with

the other, to find appropriate cues and responses to facilitate the verbal and nonverbal dialogue. As a therapist, I must create the holding environment that best releases the pent-up patient. The maintenance of this environment may require simple mirroring, confrontation, or reflection, but it always assumes an awareness of the energy moving the dialogue. Energy, in this sense, has both force and direction, and can either be invested or withdrawn. What we strive to do is to get our patients to release the energy invested in old objects and to help them to reinvest in new, fulfilling relationships and pursuits.

In conclusion, interpretations combine affective, perceptual, and cognitive responses on the part of the analyst to reorganize a patient's use of psychological space. Each therapist, I believe, must develop his or her own unique style to capture the aesthetic form of the therapeutic dialogue. Furthermore, within the limits of each analyst's style, interpretive efforts give form and organization to the transference–countertransference relationship. It is our ability to tap both primary and secondary processes that makes our interpretations effective. As with any artist, our freedom to use this dual level of consciousness will be largely determined by the depth, breadth, and firmness of our grounding in theory as well as the freedom we have to utilize our inner representational worlds in maintaining a holding environment for our patients.

If we are then able to take the emotional risk of being vulnerable with our patients, perhaps for a brief moment there can be a touch of poetry, an experience of artistry, as each participant approaches a sense of transcendence.

Postscript

Two years after this presentation, the patient reported the following dream:

> I am in a dark basement. I am lifting a 3-year-old girl up into a window where she can go into a beautiful garden. The garden is full of light and beauty. I am still in the basement, bending over a man who looks like you.

The lightness and luminosity has now entered the patient's psychic world. She is still involved with problems and fears of humiliation and submission to men, but the 3-year-old wants out and is enjoying the lush garden. The patient's fear of separation from a very powerful, destructive introject became our therapeutic direction as she approached the oedipal with both terror and hope.

Three weeks later, the patient reported a strange dream.

> I think it was a microwave oven with all types of red waves streaming out from it. It really was like a red globe. I thought immediately of the film, *Close Encounters of the Third Kind*. I don't know why I thought of this movie.

I remarked that a good deal of this glow was present in the movie as a symbol of the transformation of mankind and the birth of civilization. "Could this have anything to do with you," I asked. She was very touched and moved by my comments. She reminded me of a previous dream which had to do with fire. "You see," she said, "when I was younger, I set fire to my house." And now I said, "That fire is turning into a glow and you are becoming less frightened of love, sexuality, and hope."

A few closing comments now seem in order. Sexuality cannot be separated from the very essence and life-force of an individual. For some, in fact, this may be the only authentic expression of the self. For others, this force remains an inner glow completely compartmentalized from a more direct bodily expression. Obviously, the varieties of mergings of sexuality and life-force are numerous. For my patient, sexual expression was good. Often, however, her problems seemed to be soothed or contained in a very active form of sexual expression, which at times was an overwhelming challenge for her husband. The restriction of this life-force for my patient was often redirected by her protests of impotence and envy. Hope and transformation were absolutely buried under the specter of an extraordinary life of deprivation and despair. Now, the glimmers of a spiritual and life-giving transformation are being reborn out of some very black embers of lost dreams and frustrated wishes.

9

A Psychoaesthetic Perspective to Spirituality and Alternate Levels of Reality

This chapter originally was to appear in my most recent book, *Between Therapists: The Processing of Transference–Countertransference Material* (Robbins, 1988). At the last minute, I decided to omit this chapter even though much of the material was both moving and relevant to the subject. At the time I felt something was missing, but was unable to do any further exploration of my feelings to get a handle on the real problem. As I subsequently reviewed this material, new pieces fell into place to render a broader picture. The following tells the story both of the presenting therapist in a countertransference supervisory group and the group leader, namely myself, and our mutual personal struggles in working toward an integration of our personal and professional therapeutic selves in facing the

245

harrowing experience of watching an analytic patient die of AIDS.

The title of this chapter focuses on the concept of reality. While defining the term "reality" in any absolute sense is challenging and working with it within the context of transference–countertransference communications is difficult, we all do come to some sense of what the word means for us. The sense of it is something each of us starts to develop from birth as we move back and forth between information gained from our inner core and from "the other." This negotiation is a life-long process. Because there are at least some commonalties in our journeys from birth onward, we agree on at least some basic "realities," while others are highly idiosyncratic and personal. What is most commonly accepted is that "reality" is something tangible, logical, provable, perhaps visible and countable. What happens, then, when a therapist is faced with the possible death of a patient and must consider the notion that perhaps a normal part of human development involves disengaging from "reality" as we know it to prepare for an "alternate reality"? If one decides to follow through, then the therapeutic self must necessarily grapple with issues of the self beyond reality as we commonly know it to consider the place of spiritual issues for ourselves, for our patients, and within the therapeutic context. In taking this leap, the therapist enters a realm frequented by artists, theologians, and healers; a realm in which many levels of "reality" are accepted, the spiritual being but one.

Let us take a look now as to what as people we offer our patients. Most clearly, regardless of our theoretical orientations, patients will invariably experience our uniqueness of temperament and character structure, which invariably interfaces with transference–countertransference. This particularly includes our conceptualizations of life and death, our notions of consciousness, and our beliefs or lack thereof in the existence of other levels of reality not necessarily emanating from our family intrapsychic experiences.

Obviously there are many reality factors that a therapist brings to his patients over and above the ones just mentioned. What most immediately comes to mind are such factors as the ongoing pressures of time, money, and family responsibilities that invariably impinge upon the transference–countertransference reactions. We can further ennumerate special issues regarding women therapists, the practical considerations of professional survival, and the consideration of one's physical health, among others. These particular issues, however, have been addressed in other texts and articles. The subject of this chapter concerns itself with one particular aspect of the relationship of the professional self to reality: the impending death of one's patient and the relationship of this event to the therapist's value system, notions of life and death, and the interface of these areas with one's early relationship to illness and death.

In the following presentation, we will see the therapist's character structure and her organization of defenses being mobilized when faced with this personal emergency on the part of her patient. The therapist's solutions are unique to her, though they may be useful to other therapists. What becomes patently clear from the transcript is that such important life events as birth, illness, and death can best be faced on an existential basis, for indeed, when we face death, we are very much alone.

A therapist's solutions and experience with a dying patient presents its own therapeutic parameters that must come into contact with the therapist's professional ego ideal, the flexibility of a therapist's boundaries, and his or her theoretical notions regarding the place of gratification and responsiveness in treatment. I would like to suggest that if we perceive normal development to involve the movement from the inside to the outside, that perhaps it is also fitting to entertain the possibility that at a certain point in development there is a redirection of energy from the outside to the inside. Any number of questions arise here: Is it appropriate to reduce these notions to the struggle of life and death forces inside of us? Is it even part of our jobs as analysts to facilitate this movement from the outside to the inside? Have some patients already given up when they start treatment and we are merely onlookers as they prepare for death, or must our patients be offered the opportunity to actively grapple with their rights to live or die? Inherent in this problem is how much value we place on life regardless of one's life circumstances and how much we value conscious determination as a vital and important part of the treatment process.

In the following supervisory session, we ultimately arrive at the conclusion that at best what we have to offer a dying patient is our emotional presence and availability. Though this conclusion is patently true, I now believe that these conclusions are far too limiting. Perhaps my background as a more conservative psychoanalytic therapist may have contributed to this initially limited stance in the face of a dying patient. I recall my analyst commenting about the Jungians' belief in continuing developmental stages as we grow older that go beyond infantile sexuality. In retrospect, I now have a clearer understanding of these issues and would like to more specifically elaborate upon the area involving the impact of the spiritual self and its place in the ongoing therapy process.

To define spirituality is a tall order. I do not see myself as an expert in this area, but rather as one involved in coming to terms with basic concepts. I do experience various individuals as projecting a quality of luminosity about them; that there is a light or glow that seems to emanate from them. People seem to feel better in their presence without their having to say much about who or what they are. This inner light emanates a feeling of hope as well as peace. Perhaps within these individuals dwells a hidden knowledge of an order about life and an understanding of their place in the universe. More importantly, I sense that they have acquired an acceptance of this order and a sense of peace about it.

I have observed that many therapists have become disillusioned about the place of religion in their lives. For myself, I found no peace or connectedness with spiritual issues within the context of more formal religious institutions, and as an adult, dissociated myself from any formal religious tie. I have further observed that for me, as well as many other therapists, the analytic institute has become the new house of worship. It has offered many of us a network, a community, a feeling of belonging and security. Yet, an analytic institution and community does not offer an inner spiritual presence, for it is often political, usually educational, and sometimes godlike.

As a group leader, I struggle with these issues and present to the reader the plight of a young therapist who faces the terror of watching a young man die of AIDS.

Let us now turn to the case presentation made in a countertransference group. The presenter, Dorothy, immediately launched into a dramatic introduction. She spoke in an intensely forceful voice that sometimes slipped into a questioning self-doubt. She would maintain this intense, emotionally charged voice throughout her presentation, and the group immediately felt her tension, responding with hushed concentration.

Dorothy's framework for doing analysis was sorely shaken when her patient, Joe, announced he had AIDS and was dying. Suddenly, above and beyond such analytic issues as transference, countertransference, defenses, resistance, and infantile sexuality, Dorothy was faced with her sense of helplessness and pain regarding Joe, as well as more personal fears and defenses toward death and dying. AIDS has become the modern-day Black Plague of civilization. Some therapists are frightened of this disease and want nothing to do with patients who could possibly contaminate their protected professional world, while others respond with a sense of helplessness and despair, simply unable to deal with youth facing such an awful death. Dorothy, with the group's help, realized that the best she could do for her patient was to share the essence of herself with the recognition that true mourning could only occur where there was true relatedness unimpeded by guilt, rage, fear, or ambivalence.

Let's move into the formal presentation.

"I have a patient who is dying of AIDS. It's the second patient, really...I had one who died, and I think that I feel—I know that I feel blocked about it. Let me tell you about this case."

Affects bubbled near the surface as she spoke.

"This is a patient with whom I have worked for 6 years. I talked about him once. He is basically schizoid, whatever schizoid means. He's very withdrawn, very isolated. He has been coming twice a week for about 2 years; once a week before that." Dorothy deeply sighed then continued. "In terms of his sexuality, he's homosexual; he used to go to the baths a lot. He's never had any kind of sustained relationship. About 2 years ago, he stopped going to the baths after a bout with gonorrhea. He is also a recovering alcoholic who hasn't had a drink in about 9 years. He began talking about compulsive sex as a replacement for alcohol about the time that AIDS started to be publicized.

"Since Joe stopped going to the baths, he's had very few 'liaisons.' I don't know what to call them: very few sexual contacts, really very few. What has happened is that he began to use porn films as a sexual outlet, and he was aware of that, but he felt that at least it was safe. He was very frightened about contracting AIDS.

"Anyway, from January on, he has been complaining to me that he hasn't been able to sleep. He's been going to sleep, waking up in the middle of the night, sitting up in a chair for a few minutes, smoking until he's relaxed, then finally going back to sleep. He described incredible tension. I thought all this was connected to psychological issues, but now when I think back on it, I wonder if it wasn't a sign—maybe there were other symptoms that he wasn't describing, like night sweats or whatever—but I wonder if waking up wasn't related to AIDS. I know there's no way of knowing, but..." Dorothy's voice trailed off and she looked tortured. She took a deep breath and picked up her story.

"What I'm saying is that maybe there were other things that he wasn't describing to me. Anyway—I don't know how coherent this will be—we were really working on the way he was waking up in the middle of the night. He was very upset about it. Now, he is a very primitive guy. He's educated and very well spoken, but very infantile. When he'd talk to me, he was often unclear. There was a lot of wishing on his part that I would know what he was talking about without his having to speak in full sentences, without his having to make clear references to the particular person he was speaking about. Part of our interaction would be his giving me half a sentence and my asking him a question, pulling out the meaning of what he was saying. I tried to deal with our form of communication over the years, but we haven't gotten too far. Finally, about one or two months ago, because he was so filled with tension and was so upset about this waking up in the middle of the night, and because I so very much wanted to help him, I really did..." Again, Dorothy's voice broke and she struggled to regain her composure.

> I am aware of Dorothy's upset and pain and my struggle to stay with her feelings. I know she does not quite know what to do with her sense of impotency and helplessness. I see the beginnings of a developmental phase that will have its own particular cycle regarding Dorothy's acceptance of life and death in her patient. In the back of my mind I had my own doubts as to what I had to contribute to these awesome issues.

"Anyway, I started to confront him about his inability, no his unwillingness, to communicate. If he really wanted my help, he had to communicate. In one session, he got absolutely furious at me and went storming out of the session. I knew why he was angry at me, and for once I was able to understand the induced countertransference—I could see what I was in and how he had to get out."

> Dorothy wants the patient to deal with his feelings, from a variety of motivations. For one, she is frozen out of the patient's life and is cut off from her patient. To sit with this sense of helplessness may recapitulate the patient's early life. Both parties are alone. Is this how the patient encountered similar early life experiences?

"Now, you have to understand that he had a mother who was unbelievably intrusive. For example, part of his unwillingness or difficulty in communicating in whole sentences is because with his mother he never had to do it. Finally, when we got together again, we discussed why he had been so angry at me, his anger at my not reading his mind. He went back into his relationship with his mother and said that when they would have an argument or discussion one day, he could walk into the kitchen the next day and say 'Can I . . .' and she would say 'No,' relating to what had gone on the day before. They both knew exactly what they were talking about. That's what he wanted from me. That's why he was so angry, too. He was furious that that kind of symbiosis couldn't exist with anyone other than his mother."

> The problem of intrusiveness and invasion becomes a perplexing one in this interaction. When does reaching out and reflecting what a patient is experiencing become

an intrusion rather than empathic contact? Is the patient
defending himself against invasion or does he need
someone to break through his "stay away" stance?

"Anyway, he went storming out. That was on
Thursday. I didn't call him. After agonizing over it, I
felt I could give him the space to be angry at me, that
we needed to play it out to see what was really going on
in the transference. The next Thursday, he didn't show
up, but he called and said—in a sentence—'I'm not
going to be here today, but I'll be there on Tuesday.' In
other words, he missed a whole week of sessions.

"When he showed up the following Tuesday, I
opened the door and I was shocked by his appearance.
He's always been slight, but he looked like he'd just
come from a death camp. He told me he'd lost 25
pounds. This is somebody who couldn't afford to lose
an ounce, and I'm not exaggerating! He came in and sat
down and said that during that week he had been away
from the sessions, he also had not been able to shake a
cold that he'd had. He finally went to a doctor, and the
doctor told him he had bronchitis and gave him some
medication to take care of it. He went home, followed
instructions, but the medication wasn't working. In our
session he said, 'I guess I need a gay doctor, a doctor
who specializes in AIDS.' It was like he'd dropped a
bomb." Dorothy dissolved as she said, "I did with the
last patient what I am doing with him." She stopped to
pull herself together before she went on.

"It's like I don't want to acknowledge his dying. I
feel that I'm pushing him far away even though I did
support his going to a doctor who's experienced in
these things." Dorothy took a deep breath and continued. "With Joe's swollen nodes and weight loss, the
doctor at first thought that Joe had ARC..."

Dorothy acknowledges her state of shock and denial. She struggles with a common therapeutic response to the dying patient: In order to protect ourselves from loss we take distance from our patients and experience a vague sense of unreality. At the same time, we struggle with this denial and push ourselves to be helpful and emotionally present. I recognized that this very same process was going on in myself.

."..Which is basically AIDS related?" someone broke in to ask.

"Yes, the doctor said Joe didn't have AIDS, he did have some sort of bacterial infection, and the doctor gave him medication to cure that. Joe took that and continued with the bronchitis medication from the first doctor. None of the medication helped, so he went back to the new doctor the following week. This time the doctor took x rays. The x rays showed that he had pneumonia. Joe was given medication for pneumonia and the doctor said, 'Look, I don't have confirmation that you have AIDS, but if you respond to this particular medication, you've got it, because this medication only affects a pneumonia associated with AIDS.' Joe responded to the medication...

"You see, I'm telling you this because I don't want to believe it. I'm saying to you as I say to myself, 'It still hasn't been confirmed by the blood test.' I've even said that to him. I've been making these asshole comments...It's like I..." Again Dorothy broke down and sobbed.

Dorothy cannot face her helplessness in the face of an inevitable reality. She knows that words cannot offer her patient any solace. Yet, she cannot find in herself anything else to offer her patient. She must now face some of her own notions about life and death and her place in

the universe. Do these issues become part of the transference–countertransference relationship? Perhaps Dorothy is a container for her patient's pain. Maybe she can
also be a conduit of hope, for in the end there must be
some light in all this darkness. As I think this, I am not
too secure with these notions for I struggle with my
own understanding of the larger order of the universe
and my place in it.

"Anyway, the whole point is that because I don't
want to believe it, I can't really help him. Yesterday I
talked to him, and that's when I realized he's very sick.
A friend of mine who works at a drug clinic in a hospital said, 'You know, once they get pneumonia, their
time is really very short, even though the doctor said
that treatment could help.' So I'm hoping that maybe he
has a year or two."

We see a slow, grudging acceptance that death is around
the corner. Now there is a compromise; maybe he has a
year or two to go.

"Yesterday I saw him and he said to me: 'For the
first time I feel really sick. I haven't even thought about
dying before, but now I'm going through this awful
medication...' And then, the next thing he told me was
that he thought he'd get rid of his dog who's about 13
years old. What he *said* was that his dog wasn't responding to signals anymore and was sleeping a lot. It
was too hard for him."

After a long pause Dorothy said, "It's what Joe is
doing that's distressing to me. He has talked to a friend
and the friend has said he would take the dog and put
him to sleep. Now Joe is a very angry man, very rigid
and controlled, and I am afraid to deal with him too
much, because I don't want him exploding at me. I am
so conflicted about all this and yet I didn't want to say

too much about the dog. So I simply said, 'Well, are you sure about this?' He said 'Yes, I *am* sure, and I think my friend is going to do it.' I don't know, but I'm thinking that the dog is not ready to die...Joe and the dog together..."

> The symbolic meaning of putting the dog to sleep explodes in Dorothy's head. Questions equally erupt in my head. The patient is already preparing himself for death. Do we, as therapists, insist that patients fight for life? Do we help them maintain their life connections, or is there some inner decision that patients unconsciously make as to whether to live or die? Do we insist that patients make this an active rather than a passive choice?

Dorothy's voice was reaching a high pitch. "What is he doing? What is he acting out? I don't really know if I'm even going to see this guy again. The doctor said that he is responding well to the medication, but then I think of what my friend said, and I would like to care a little more for him than I did with my other AIDS patient.

"When my first patient told me he was dying of AIDS, I didn't know what he was talking about. For a year they couldn't diagnose him and he had all the symptoms: He had been sick constantly, acquiring venereal diseases, one illness after another. I remember him saying, 'I think I have AIDS.' And my thinking, 'What are you talking about?' I'd never heard of it.

"Then finally they *did* diagnose him. All the publicity also started coming out, and I understood what he had been talking about. And he died three months later. Once he got too weak to come in and he was hospitalized, I talked to him daily. The way I handled it was to be as available as I could be on the telephone.

But I never went to see him, which I feel guilty about. I rationalized it by saying that he wouldn't have wanted me to come see him. He was very proud; he wouldn't have wanted me to see him looking the way he did. There were all sorts of things I never really even offered—I was scared.

> I keep on asking myself: What do we offer our patients when they are in the process of dying? Perhaps Dorothy feels betrayed by her dying patient for there are secret rescue fantasies and magical solutions that invariably surround the people who are left on earth to deal with the mourning process. Did we do enough; do we rescue our patient from death so that we do not personally have to feel lost? Secretly we are relieved that it is not us who are dying and are upset and ashamed of such feelings. Sometimes we are insulated from our patient, for we do not want to be contaminated by the specter of death. Most importantly, we are inwardly confused as to the meaning of life and death. I am aware that these questions are my attempt to insulate *myself* from this painful presentation, for it feels all too overwhelming to take in.

"I felt terrible, the way he died. The whole year afterward, I dreamed about him. I really mourned." Dorothy sobbed uncontrollably. Finally she began talking as though there was a force pushing her to get this material out.

"I feel like I abandoned him, even though I don't believe I did. Anyway, I don't want to abandon Joe, but I see it coming. I won't abandon him physically, I'll be there, but I'm afraid I'll abandon him emotionally..." A long pause followed. The room was absolutely quiet with a circle of intensely sad faces turned toward Dorothy. All of us knew of Dorothy's conflict with her previous patient who ironically had referred Joe for treatment.

Our mutual guilt regarding the resentment that is directed toward the dying patient may well be in operation here. Consciously Dorothy feels that she has abandoned her patient, but on the latent level, is it the other way around?

"You don't want to abandon him," Denise reiterated.

"No, but I'm afraid I will—like I abandoned Henry—I'm on the verge of abandoning Joe, and I don't want to do that. I just keep trying to say optimistic things, like my family does when somebody is sick. My family is very optimistic around illness. There's a 'You can get better' attitude. Even when somebody was dying in front of our eyes, my family would always say, 'You're going to get better.' I don't say to Joe, 'You're going to get better,' I'm better than t'at, but I say things like, 'The doctor hasn't given you a diagnosis.' He says to me, 'The doctor told me that I would respond to the medication if I have AIDS.' I mean, Joe isn't supposed to take care of *me* through this."

Sharing real feelings between a dying patient and therapist is a most complex business. We often protect the dying patient from our real feelings and as a result they may, at times, feel isolated. In the face of a critical physical illness, we are angry at our platitudes, but do we dare deal with more direct feelings?

A long pause followed until someone, in a low, soft, supportive voice, broke the silence. "Maybe he wants you to cheer him up. I don't think it sounds like he wants you to deny the disease, because he *is* saying 'I have it.' So, what would happen if you discussed it with him? Is there something that he wants from you?"

> This patient may not be able to say what he wants from
> Dorothy. However, it certainly is a good starting point.
> If nothing else, we will hear from the patient what he is
> ready to deal with in terms of death and illness.

Another long pause followed and finally Dorothy spoke. "You know, I've been so wrapped up in it, it never dawned on me. I think it would be fine for me to ask him that directly. I told him I wanted to be involved in this, that I wanted to know what was happening. But it never dawned on me to ask him what he wants from me."

Daisy continued in a somber tone. "The frame is changed now, since he cannot come to see you. How are you going to adjust the frame?"

"He wants telephone contact, that I know. I've kept that. He calls me at a set time."

"He calls you at the session time? Is that how it works?" someone asked.

"Yes, not the whole time; 15 minutes, 20 minutes. I presume it will be longer as he's ready to deal with his feelings."

> The telephone becomes an important modification of
> therapeutic structure. The drawback with using this
> method of contact often revolves around our compul-
> sion to talk rather than leave empty spaces in a tele-
> phone conversation. Both parties will have to face that
> the use of the telephone does not mean they have to be
> social, but can remain therapeutic.

I knew we had to plunge deeper. We had no choice, so I asked, "So how does this connect with your background?"

> I heard myself speaking and bit my tongue, as my com-
> ment seemed hollow and analytic. I knew that this topic
> was getting to me by the sound of my voice.

"Well, I know what it's about. My whole life has been connected with heart disease and death, and the only way I've come through has been to live day by day. I remember coming to that conclusion years ago. My mother had bypass surgery twice plus a couple of heart attacks; my father had a heart attack. Everybody dies from heart disease in my family—even my sister's cat died of a heart attack! Anyway, I remember as a teenager the doctor telling me that my mother was dying and it was then that I made the decision to live day to day. That was it. That has been it, and that's what I'm doing now with this patient."

After another long silence Dorothy continued. "My fantasy is that I should be talking to Joe about his feelings, about his disease, although he's told me he's not ready to talk about them. He's been too sick to think about his feelings. And then there's this whole thing with the dog. I still feel that I should have suggested he wait to make a decision about the dog until he was feeling better. He *will* feel better. It will go up and down for a while, I assume."

> We observe how the uniqueness of Dorothy's life experience interfaces with the problems of her patient. These personal issues cannot merely be reduced to unresolved infantile issues. The therapist has her scars and has learned to live with the dread of sudden illness that surrounds her family history. The anxiety and living on tenterhooks can not easily be dispensed by the decision to live day by day with this reality. Can Dorothy now live with her patient's character problems that will invariably make him less accessible and more frightened, at least for the time being?

More silence enveloped the group before someone said, "But he is going to kill the dog."

"Because he's afraid of not being able to take care of it." Shifting abruptly, Dorothy then said, "I know that this is crazy, but somehow with his getting up in the middle of the night, I feel that I should have known..."

A hubbub of voices answered with, "This is crazy!"

"It's related to the symbiotic fear," Daisy said in slow measured tones.

"What if you had known?" someone asked. "Let's assume that somehow you had the power to know, what would have happened?"

Dorothy talked slowly, her voice cracking under the strain. "Maybe I could have helped him to begin to deal with it earlier, gotten him to a doctor earlier...I have no idea...I just feel that I should be there to help him with his feelings—that there is a process a patient goes through, and that somehow I should help him to do that before he dies."

> All of us tend to resort to magical thinking when we are faced with our personal helplessness and impotence in our response to death. We must do something if only to avoid the dread of the unknown. Is there something beyond this, such as an inner certainty that there is a rhyme and reason to life and death and a greater order to life around us? Certainly such a belief might be of enormous help in this most difficult situation. We do not have to talk about our notions of life and death; it is the projection of an inner attitude that goes beyond words that we feel and sense in another. I hear my colleagues replying to these questions with, 'The only meaning that there is out there is what we place on it; otherwise it is chaos.' I wonder how this conviction will carry them through.

Dolores now pointed out in low, soothing tones:

"This is also the sort of man who has great difficulty locating his feelings. You were beginning to press him and you encountered a lot of rage, so in some ways, it seems that you are idealizing what you're going to get. You need him to help you with your mourning process, but he may not be able to go through it quite that way, especially now that he's kind of withdrawn and sick."

Dorothy reflected a moment before answering. "I know what you're saying. I think you're right. I think it's hard to know. I feel confused, and maybe I *am* asking him to do what he can't do. There's a part of me that is afraid of him because of all that rage underneath. I mean, who's going to get it?" The tears streamed from Dorothy's eyes as she talked. "He has said to me a couple of times on the phone, 'My life has been such a complete waste.' It hasn't been a waste, but I know he's had a difficult life, a tough time. He had a mother who was unbelievable and his father abandoned him emotionally. I guess I'm angry—at his potential to grow, at least in my fantasies, and what didn't work." She cried and slowly regained her composure. "It's not fair!" Deep silence reigned.

> Dorothy enters another phase in her struggle to accept death. She denies, compromises, and is enraged. There are no neat answers that fit into traditional conflict theory. Do we dare entertain such "far-out" notions as a person completing his mission on earth? Certainly these ideas do not fit with the pragmatic, reality-oriented perception that is so pervasive in our culture and society. Even with the acceptance of the thought that a patient has no longer a reason to live, do we have an obligation to help patients discover new reasons for staying here in this reality?

"I feel I've failed," said Dorothy softly. "I just feel

like the most innocent people...it feels like they're the children of the world, they're the most helpless ones— They get it."

Daisy reflected: "I guess they do feel like children. That's true."

Eleanor alluded to Kubler-Ross's work, and Dorothy responded: "I haven't done any reading about it, although I ought to, I suppose. The thing is I don't want to impose my agenda. I've got to be careful. On the other hand, suppose he never wants to talk about it. Do I insist on it? How can I insist?"

"If you insist," Leonore said in a high-pitched voice, "He can say no! Did you feel you were acting out when you demanded that he finish his sentences?"

Dorothy emphatically responded: "Yes, I did, I do. I also have this idealized image of what an analyst does."

"What's that?" probed Leonore.

Dorothy sobbed: "Somebody else would have said something that I didn't...Some calm, easy interpretation about not finishing sentences that would have unlocked doors...I wish I had the power to control Joe's physical being, and I know I don't, but..."

I started to intervene by saying, "Maybe we can offer a mirror of what Joe is going through. Perhaps sharing some of these feelings is important so that he will not feel alone."

Cybil concurred, "It's very normal for him to struggle and deny some of these feelings."

Denise added, "When you talked to me last night about the case, you said 'This is the last time that I am taking a gay patient because they die on me.'"

Dorothy responded, as though confessing, "I am

furious. I cry so much, and I feel selfish sitting here and talking to the group about this. I'm talking about me, about my mourning process, and I feel like I should be talking about Joe."

> Another element creeps into the picture. Do any of us dare deal with his individual existence when his patient is being robbed of life? One's personal guilt is profound and secretly hides in dark crevices creating self-attacks from an inner sense of fairness and authority.

Denise responded pointedly: "When has anybody else presented a case where she's not talking about herself?"

Dolores shared some of her concerns. "I have two patients right now who are in a similar situation. One patient is dying, and I've been sitting here thinking about how much I am in a state of denial. I keep trying to demand that she come to sessions and she is telling me all over the place how she can't walk for half a block without being completely out of breath. I should be doing phone sessions instead of demanding that she come. It's such a hard issue, probably the hardest one we have to deal with."

"But let's look at some of the personal issues you're bringing to the case," I said. "Do you resent your parents for their heart conditions?"

"I was just thinking of that," Dorothy said, "I have never allowed myself to do that, to allow myself to resent them and to deal with the fact that they might die. I guess it's hooked up to the anger about all the other things I'm angry about and wouldn't allow myself to be openly angry about because I'm afraid I'd explode. In the past, there was always the danger that they would deprive me of their physical presence. I guess there's also a fear that if I got really angry I'd bring on a heart attack. There's a part of me that's afraid of dealing with this with Joe, because I'm afraid he's going to get angry."

> Dorothy begins to sort out her feelings regarding the transference–countertransference relationship. The anger, but more importantly the guilt, makes it very difficult for her to deal with a feeling of deprivation regarding a loss of a dying parent or patient.

"Are you afraid that he might kill himself?" someone asked.

"I don't think he would do it overtly, but I'm afraid he will throw in the towel and stop trying by not taking the medication."

I pushed provocatively. "Suppose he makes the decision that he'd rather die quickly than slowly?"

"Well," Dorothy responded, "I certainly know he has the right, and I couldn't blame him. But I would like...I guess in my family everybody has always fought to live, although I do understand that people have the right to do whatever they have to do."

> We begin to touch upon Dorothy's value system and its impact on the treatment process. If we identify with the importance and sanctity of life, do we fight for every patient's right to remain in this world? How much do we play God in identifying with a patient who feels that it is too much to maintain existence on this planet? I assume every therapist must make his/her own individual judgment regarding this matter. We must at least recognize that for some, an active decision to die may be a final act of self-affirmation, particularly if they live under extreme physical illness. For this patient, however, it appears that he has given up very early in life, indeed, long before he was physically ill.

In a supportive voice I said, "There are times when they just say 'enough is enough.'"

"I know that," Dorothy quickly answered. "This is a gray area for me. I can't quite see where my needs get confused with his, and so I end up being paralyzed."

"What are your needs?" Daisy quizzed.

"I'm paralyzed," Dorothy responded, "so I say nothing. I don't support him."

> The intensity of affects in the room was overwhelming me, and I was beginning to expect that I might be provocative as a way of warding off pain.

In any event, I said, "What's your need to keep Joe?"

Daisy spoke for Dorothy. "My fantasy is that you feel you must make him fight, to have him work this through rather than give up."

"On the other hand," I said, "treatment may help people die."

Dorothy laughed nervously. "That's what I'm trying to do, but he's supposed to go through a process in order to do that." Fear started flowing again as she continued, "But I want to be able to save his body—*that's* my fantasy—but I also want him to choose to die if that's what he wants. I have to work up to that. I can't say it tomorrow, I'm not ready."

> I can understand Dorothy's wish for the patient to *actively* choose to die. I also know that the patient may never be able to articulate his decision for he is entitled to choose his course as he lived, secretly and disconnected, both from himself and others.

"I never had a chance to say goodbye to my other patient who died of AIDS. I'm feeling so bad. When Henry got very sick, toward the end, he had to be in the hospital all the time, I never went to say goodbye. I just didn't have the nerve, and then in the last week when I was planning to be gone for a week, I didn't have the nerve to tell him. Every night I called him, but I didn't tell him I was going away. The night before I left I told him and he did his cheery routine. I guess he was furious."

"What did you tell him?" Dolores asked.

"I would be gone for a few days, I would be back, and would talk to him when I came back. He said 'fine.' When I came back he was in a coma. He died in a few days, and I guess I got furious at myself. I feel I was such a chicken shit about that." Dorothy spoke in self-berating tones: "And that's where I really fall down from my fantasy of a therapist—that I didn't have the guts to handle the whole thing."

> Dorothy continues to berate herself. Once again, we suspect that she may be overidentified with her patient and now must face some of her own introjected hostility that is secretly directed at the abandoning patient. I also know that it is virtually impossible not to mobilize our defenses under this stressful situation.

Denise shot back, "If you had told him a week ahead of time, maybe he *couldn't* have gotten angry at you. What makes you think he *would* have gotten angry at you?"

"I don't know."

On the same track, Leonore continued, "So you could have said goodbye. How did he know he was going into a coma in two weeks instead of four? That's the problem about saying goodbye. You don't know when someone is going to die unless he's suicidal and you're supporting that."

Dorothy agreed, "That's right."

Cybil added: "You assume that it would have been better for him to know you were going. Maybe it would have been just the opposite; maybe his knowing that you were there, not anticipating your leaving, was better."

> Cybil places emphasis on a most important issue. Dying patients do not necessarily want to inflict their pain upon others. Consequently, dying patients often wait until close personal friends or relatives are not physically present to die. Some patients, in fact, need permission from their loved ones to die.

"That was in the back of my mind," Dorothy confessed. "That was half of the argument, but then I couldn't make up my mind and I decided that I chickened out."

The group joined in supporting Dorothy. Cybil commented: "I've had contact with my homosexual patients who flirt around and do all kinds of self-destructive things sexually. I want to get out. I can't stand listening to it."

> We are once again approaching the gray area of survival and self-destructiveness. For many homosexual patients, promiscuousness has been a way of making contact while maintaining a safe distance from others. With AIDS, the risks have been compounded; yet for many, there is no choice but to hungrily reach out in order to make life possible. As therapists, we emotionally invest in our patients' lives and painfully must both understand this search for life and flirtation with death.

Dolores added: "But I can see why you would be especially upset. You didn't get a chance to say goodbye to your patient for yourself."

"It's not always such a neat package," someone

added, and another voice chimed in: "I was thinking, you only finally say goodbye when you can afford it. I can remember working in the hospital with dying kids, and how it helped me, somehow, to feel that I was prepared. Then I'd go back on Monday and they were still there—that's the whole issue—it really knocks you out."

"You're raising an extremely significant point," I said. "Saying goodbye is not a one-shot deal, and it isn't over in one session."

"Maybe I don't understand how to say goodbye," Dorothy reflected.

"Well," I said, "you're talking about mourning. It can go on over months, or even years. It's sometimes thinking you see your patient in the street, that's part of saying goodbye."

Cybil added: "I've often thought that if I cried a little more, I would receive relief and maybe closure wouldn't take me by surprise, that somehow I could protect myself."

> Cybil touches on the very essence of the mourning process. It is not one big catharsis, but a series of many goodbyes that cannot be rushed or purged.

Leonore broke in: "It's also related to the idea of the perfect therapist who comes up with this perfect interpretation that opens all the doors. I think the fantasy of a goodbye is that you would have said it the way you meant to say it, you wouldn't have been an asshole last week. When you never know when it's coming, you never have the chance to present yourself exactly the way you want."

"You're both putting your fingers on important issues about saying goodbye," I noted. "If you stay in a constant state of readiness to say goodbye, it's like you're constantly in a state of preparing to mourn and you never mourn. Somewhere in the back of your mind you are ready for a shock that doesn't come. This means you're always in a state of shock."

> We often prepare ourselves for the impending death of a good friend or patient by entering the mourning process even before the person dies. Yet, if we are constantly in a state of preparedness, the anxiety and sadness becomes a way of life as we are propelled into a state of constant readiness and fear. This ultimately becomes a burden and an intrusion into our own autonomy.

Dorothy now reflected: "You know my father died very suddenly. He was in the hospital, one of the millions of times that he was in the hospital, and he died. I keep going over my last contact with him. I'm just so relieved I saw him that day and that we didn't have an argument. I keep going over and over and over that visit, and I've reassured myself in some way."

"I have another question," I said. "Because your parents were always under threat of death, were you trying to magically control this upsetting situation? Did you have the fantasy that if you would be good, you could control the possibility of their death?"

Dorothy thought awhile and answered: "What I acted out was my being the caretaker of the two of them. My father was up-front about his position. I would try to make him go to the doctor, make him watch his diet. My mother's always taken good care of herself, but my father went wild; he was active in the world, he had a terrific time in life. It was also an extreme strain on him in many ways, and when I would yell at him about his not taking care of himself, he always told me, 'Look, I know what I have to do to take care of myself, and I also want to live my life. It's my nature to be out there and to have a good time—that's what I want.' I guess I hadn't thought of it from that perspective. When he said that, *that's* when I stopped having fights with him about going to the doctors. That's it. That's where I stopped. I don't know whether I stopped inside, but I stopped trying to control him."

"Suppose this patient," I probed, "said to you: 'Look I have to live my last days the way I want. I know what I am doing. This is the best alternative for me, even if this leads to my dying sooner.'"

"If he said that to me," Dorothy responded, "I would let go. It's like when patients want to retreat. If they are acting out and they want to leave, I can understand that, but in order for me to make peace with it, they have to finally say to me: 'Look, I understand I am acting out, but I am taking responsibility.' I feel responsible, and they have to let me off the hook."

> We want our patients to take responsibility for their lives. Does this therapeutic wish become a flimsy rationalization to cover an attempt to avoid feelings of guilt regarding the patient's death?

"Here's the added complication," I said. "Joe doesn't have very many verbal tools to describe his experience. You may very well have to help him with this. I guess you're worried about putting words in his mouth."

"Yes," Dorothy admitted, nodding her head and looking pained.

"So that's the dilemma," I said. "This patient doesn't really talk too much, but acts out. The only way you make contact with him is helping with words for his actions and by being mothering, caring, reflective, and mirroring."

Dolores quickly blurted out: "Killing the dog is a dilemma I can see him putting into words. He is getting ready to die. He's not going to be there to take care of his dog, so in a way it's an act of mercy that he's putting the dog away, since it's 13 years old."

I reflected out loud: "I'm just thinking about the role of a mourning ritual, like the religious wake. Traditionally, a mourning wake has something to do with a community sharing the loss. All of us have tremendous difficulty in sharing and going through the emotional work. I suspect each one of us handles it differently."

> The group becomes a holding community; a place where therapists help one another and commiserate in the sharing of common feelings. We therapists require these support groups, for in our profession, death and pain are not infrequent visitors to our office. We must develop our own modern-day rituals that will be the shock absorbers to permit us to go on as professionals.

Leonore reflected: "There are no neat answers, and I know the best experiences I've had were when there was some acknowledgment of what was going on; when I was allowed to express my feelings." Her voice was soft and low as she continued. "I remember, with one kid who died, I went to the funeral. I'll never forget—two minutes after she died, I walked in the room. I wanted to be there, and it was a very helpful thing. The most helpful part was the crying beforehand; something about the whole family sharing."

"Were you scared at first about this whole experience of dying?"

"Yes!" Leonore affirmed strongly.

Denise said by contrast: "I guess seeing it over and over again in the hospital helped me to master my fear of death. For me, being on a cancer ward was a way to learn about life."

Daisy spoke in a somber voice: "I had two patients who died. One cancer patient was very lonely, very sick. I remember talking with the doctor, the lawyer, his family—the whole painful process."

"I wonder," I said, "is there the feeling, here, that dying is really one more stage of life?"

"That's what I want and don't want to believe," Dorothy said.

> Dorothy faces her own confusion regarding a spiritual connection to the universe. In each of us, there may well be a spiritual connection that only needs permission and opportunity to realize itself. However, for all of us, this is no easy matter, and cannot simply be earned by observing a religious ritual. I know that this is very true for myself.

Dolores said with obvious pain: "That's what I've struggled with, especially with one patient who didn't want to live. I felt rageful at times, and I'd get forceful. I would have felt a lot better if she'd let me in. It was not being let in that felt so awful."

"Well *that*'s what I said to this patient one day," Dorothy said. "He was kind of hesitant, and he asked whether or not he should call again on Tuesday. I said absolutely, that I wanted to hear from him and I wanted to be involved every step of the way. Then, after I hung up, I thought to myself, 'You're not getting rid of me that easily.'"

I now tried to generalize for the group. "When you're facing issues around life and death, there is something more than analysis. You become involved in the existential questions of the nature of one's existence, the meaning of life, one's ultimate aloneness. It's absurd to think you can put everything into the framework of analysis."

"I know that," Dorothy said, "but I'm scared, and in some way the framework is safer." After a thoughtful silence she continued. "I'm afraid of being rejected. He's a very schizoid man, frightened of any contact. I want desperately to be involved and to help."

"But you may have to help him in his way," I said gently, "supporting the way he has been in life. He will not be able to share too much. He may die the way he lived, which is a little closed off, not being able to say too much. You may share some of your feelings with him, but he may not be able to do much but listen."

"Then I feel that I'm imposing my feelings," protested Dorothy.

> Dorothy has been so burdened by her family's history of physical illness that intrusion has been a very sensitive issue in her work with patients. She will soon know if the sharing of some of her feelings will in fact be an intrusion into her patient's life by his response to her emotional probing. Our answer in these instances can always be reduced to a basic pragmatic axiom: As for a particular intervention, what happens to the therapeutic process?

"No, don't worry," I said in a reassuring voice. "If he doesn't want to listen, it will bounce off him." Shifting to a more clinical position, I said, "With schizoid people, a typical transference–countertransference is 'stay away, but come close to me. Reach out and make contact with the most intimate part of me, but don't touch me.' You hear their needs, and you want to respond to their needs, but you have to be constantly aware that as much as they want to be touched, they also fear intrusion."

"That's what happened in the last session," Dorothy interjected.

I continued: "Make contact with him and let him reject you. In spite of his rejecting you, something of you will gradually come through. If you're too worried about your own aggressiveness with schizoid individuals and treat them too carefully, it can end with a final rejection because they don't have the tools to say 'come close to me.' They've got to hear it from you. You've got to do your best to be there and let the chips fall where they may."

When I stopped speaking I felt the charged atmosphere and decided to accept it directly. "Let's talk a little more about what's going on here," I said. "Death is such a loaded topic."

Rachel spoke with pain in her voice: "I tell you, I was really surprised by my reaction when my friend, a close friend, was diagnosed with breast cancer. She had surgery. Now she's been through lots of therapy, she knows her feelings, she feels good to talk to about it. So I knew that if I wanted to be there I could be there with her and she'd tell me what she needed. What surprised me was that I was so pissed. I mean, I don't have time for this! How dare she get cancer now or whenever! It really surprised me that I could feel this way, but it was there. I even told her how pissed off I was that she was sick then and she understood that. It didn't seem to hurt anything at all. She didn't stop calling me or anything, although she's not inundating me with calls either—she doesn't do that—but if I call her she'll talk for half an hour. Still, it's 'Oh shit! I don't want to go through this with her. I don't want to lose her. I don't want to feel the pain. I don't want to think about my own death. I don't want to think about the deaths I have already dealt with.' It's a pain in the ass!"

> Rachel now becomes a mirror for Dorothy's dilemma. She voices her resentment at the intrusion as well as the burden that seems to invade her inner psychic sanctuary as she works with her patient.

I added, "Many people see death as being the end. There's no spiritual base, no sense of something universal."

Leonore added her feelings. "My brother was very ill when I was a child. It was a borderline case of whether he was going to make it or not. I think that's why I went to work with leukemic children. Now it's not such an issue, the hanging on a thread about somebody's life or death, and I think a lot of it was exposure, being with other people who were dealing with it also. And then, I remember when my ex-analyst died. It was sudden, he had a heart attack. I went to the session and the doorman told me he had had a heart attack. At least it was sudden from my perspective. Art later told me my analyst had this disease for a long time, and Art knew about it for a long time. *That's* another issue entirely, but he had decided to live his life to the end, and he gave me every session he could."

"Did you know that he was sick?" someone asked.

> I think that our patients invariably know when something very profound is happening to the therapist. For some therapists, like Leonore's, however, keeping this material out of the treatment becomes part of their own professional integrity. In Leonore's case, the sharing of

this material *would* have been an enormous burden for
Leonore to carry.

"I asked him more than once," Leonore said.

"He didn't want to give you that burden," I said.

"I know that he wanted to give me the opportunity
to work with him as an analyst."

Dolores now shared her experience. "When I had
this foot surgery, I made it into this whole big thing. I
struggled with whether I was going to prepare people
for this or come in with my foot bandaged. It was really
a small thing, but it wasn't. I felt I had to do the preparation on a case-by-case basis. There was one little girl I
felt I really needed to prepare, while for some others,
they needed to do their work. For them, this was of
really little consequence, not really something to focus
on it at that point."

> We see how patients will often offer us direction as to
> how and when we share our private thoughts and feel-
> ings with our patients. Listening to our patients, then,
> and following their clues can give us enormous help as
> to which way to turn as we are faced with the dilemma
> of violating the patient's privacy or intruding into his
> sense of isolation.

Leonore added: "I think, also, it's very important
to be able to make a mistake. This was true in the hospital with the dying kids and also for my analyst who
died. He did what he did, in good faith, and I've had to
deal with it."

I tried to sum up. "The most precious gift you have
to offer your dying patient is to make contact in any
way you know, with your anger, your upset, your
worry, your denial, and then simply 'be' with that
other person."

> Perhaps at a later point in my development, I would have interjected the topic of spirituality, for the act of being with a patient, particularly in these circumstances, may well demand conveying an inner sense of peace and knowledge of the order of life. For many therapists this knowledge does not come easily and may never be integrated into a professional therapeutic self. I suspect, however, that the most appropriate therapist for the dying patient may well be one who has integrated a spiritual self into his professional work with a dying patient.

"Perhaps that makes me feel better," Dorothy said. "I'm feeling a little more comfortable in the ups and downs, and I really feel that any time I need to, I can talk about these issues. Maybe that's what it's all about; it's *not* just about the patient. Thank you."

The group quietly and reflectively left the room.

In Dorothy's work with Joe, a rather withdrawn schizoid individual, her personal relatedness and emotional presence may be a most important source of support offered to Joe in the treatment relationship. As in many areas of treatment, a paradox exists, for while in early development we travel from the inside to the outside, in death we move from the outside inward. For this schizoid patient who has remained all too inward during the course of his life, Dorothy is faced with the challenge of offering her emotional presence as an ally in the transcendent journey from life to death, at the same time respecting the patient's right to die as he lived.

Dorothy must also face her own trials and tribulations regarding the mourning process, and recognize that it can never be done within one session. Mourning, for all of us, becomes a process of saying goodbye.

This process takes place over months if not years. The reliving of images of the past and the emotional letting go simply takes time. It's good to be aware of the subtle distinction here between the processes of the mourning connected to loss and melancholia. As we review our experience of mourning, there is much less pain and ambivalence. By contrast, where the lost relationship becomes embedded with feelings of guilt, rage, fear, helplessness, and pained ambivalence, saying goodbye becomes a very difficult process. The lost object is no longer outside of oneself, but internalized through an introjective process. By swallowing what is unpalatable and undigestible, we avoid the pain of our ambivalence and consequently cannot separate enough from the object to say goodbye. For Dorothy, the intrusion of her family's illness interfered with the separation–individuation process and consequently made her all too vulnerable to depression. Exploring the countertransference ambivalence that retards the mourning process of a dying patient becomes the emotional work of a therapist. Occasionally a patient's death is met with countertransference numbness by the therapist. Somewhere that patient is buried within the therapist's ego like a foreign body that requires a more appropriate burial place. Dorothy feels cheated and robbed of accompanying her patient through the mourning process.

There will be further work for Dorothy's professional therapeutic self in grappling with these very important issues regarding spirituality and the meaning of life, both philosophically and as it affects her presence in sessions. For Dorothy, the meaning of death has been filtered through her personal history involving living in a constant state of readiness to experience loss. This, in turn, has added to her sense of personal deprivation and abandonment on the one hand, guilt and hopelessness on the other. Underlying it all has been the need to control this whole sphere, and a deep reservoir of anger and resentment. At the same time, Dorothy is faced with the question of how she can maintain an angry stance with the father when an emotional confrontation can create a heart attack. The fear of becoming too direct or assertive is carried into her work with patients. How easily Dorothy makes peace with these conflicts so that she is available to enter into an unconflicted mourning process with seriously ill patients remains to be seen.

The death of a patient often touches the most primitive layers of a therapist's personality structure. We react with dread and feelings of vulnerability as we easily place ourselves in our patients' shoes. At times we can experience ourselves searching along with the patient for a magical interpretation that will make the transitional stage from life to death a less painful one.

Some of us are tempted to emotionally disengage from our patients before they die, if only to insulate ourselves from the shock of loss. Others may plunge into an overidentification with a dying patient and are thrown into a panic state, fearing that we too will die with our patient. For many, the notion of death touches upon a sense of inner disintegration rather than a state of transition. This fear is compounded when we watch our patient's body disintegrate over weeks if not days. None of us really know what happens to us after death, and at best we have only an inner conviction that can be neither substantiated nor denied. In the end, we find there's no way out of facing the affects of pain and loss, regardless of faith issues.

There are no perfect ways to handle such primitive anxieties or deep inner convictions about the meaning of life or death. At best, we must call on a mastery of our defenses to understand the impact of an impending death of a patient so that we can prepare ourselves to be emotionally present as allies during this most difficult passage.

As I have had time to reflect on my discomfort with how the session reported in this chapter ended, I am struck with the interfacing of therapeutic and healing–spiritual–cosmic issues. On the one hand, I recognize the importance of clear process and transference–countertransference issues like those we worked on with Dorothy and those not touched on but running beneath the surface of such cases, like our fears of contamination on both psychological and physiological levels and our need to be honest with ourselves and our clients regarding boundaries. Closer to the fine line between therapeutic and spiritual issues, however, is the importance of working with "forgiveness." All too many AIDS patients see their illness as a punishment for what society has labeled their "dirtiness" or "promiscuity," but this begs the issue of facing the larger order of things. Underneath this "easy answer" may be an immense rage, or fear of rage, at the therapist as representing parent–society–God for not saving them from this awful disease. Therapy can be a context to help these patients to face their mortality, perhaps more grisly, but no more or less real than that of all of us; to find forgiveness for not being rescued, for finding some light and a larger meaning.

Of course, to do this, we as therapists must first look within ourselves and struggle with our own understanding of life and death, spirituality, and alternate realities. As I write this, I vaguely recognize that my analytic self feels embarrassed and uncomfortable in approaching cosmic issues, for Freudian thinking offers little room for such notions. At the same time, I am not comfortable with Freud's answers when faced with momentous life and death issues. Where does this leave us? I believe that we have something very special to offer our patients other than our personal presence and relatedness, and I also recognize that I may be crossing the boundary between a spiritual healer and a therapist in this belief. This line is still vague in my mind, but it will become an increasingly important question and "line" to address as I, as well as other therapists, are increasingly faced with patients dying from AIDS. We will be forced to ask ourselves: Is death the end, or is there more to life than the mere confines of one's personal existence, of imposing our unique senses of order on apparent chaos? Certainly the meaning of death transcends the material of infantile sexuality as traditionally emphasized in analytic treatment. It seems to me that just as we are called on to deal with the earliest, most primary issues of mother and child at one end of the life cycle, we can no longer ignore looking at the transition from life to death with its profound implications for treatment.

If we do believe that death is but one more transition to another level of consciousness, then joining our patients in this "no boundary" level of existence may be a choice for every therapist to make. As this book draws to an end, I continue to explore the relationship of form and formlessness, leaving open the possibility for an integration of a healing/spiritual approach within a psychoanalytic perspective. In psychotherapy, the interplay of form and formlessness, or self and other, can be observed through the therapeutic holding relationship and the therapist's interpretive intervention. In healing, the same relationship between form and formlessness takes place but on a different level of reality. Perhaps in all cases there is a time for healing and a place for intrapsychic organization. Hopefully this text has made a small contribution in joining the healer, the artist, and the scientist in the practice of psychoanalytic psychotherapy.

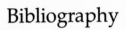

Bibliography

References

Aristotle (1957). *Politics* and *Poetics*. New York: Viking Press.

Arnheim, R. (1982). *The power of the center.* Los Angeles: University of California Press.

Artaud, A. (1958). *The theatre and its double.* New York: Grove Press.

Behrends, R. S., & Blatt, S. N. (1985). Internalization and psychological development through the life cycle. In A. J. Solnit, R. S. Essler, & P. B. Newbauer (Eds.), *The psychoanalytic study of the child.* New Haven: Yale University Press.

Bollas, C. (1987). *The shadow of the object: Psychoanalysis of the unthought known.* New York: Columbia University Press.

Boomer, D. S. (1978). The phonemic clause: Speech unit in human communication. In *Nonverbal behavior and communication*. Hillsdale, NJ: Lawrence Erlbaum Associates.

Brecht, B. (1948). *Parables for the theatre*. New York: Grove Press.

Clynes, M. (1977). *Sentics—The touch of emotions*. Garden City, NY: Anchor Press, Doubleday.

Clynes, M. (Ed.) (1982). *Music, mind, and brain—the neurophysiology of music*. New York: Plenum Press.

Cole, D. (1975). *The theatrical event*. Middletown, CT: Wesleyan University Press.

Confer, W. (1987). *Intuitive psychotherapy*. New York: Human Sciences Press.

Condon, W. S. (1982). Cultural microrhythms. In M. Davis (Ed.), *Interaction rhythms: Periodicity in communicative behavior*. New York: Human Sciences Press.

Deikman, A. (1973). Biomodal consciousness. In R. Ornstein (Ed.), *The nature of human consciousness*. San Francisco: W. H. Freeman & Co.

Ehrenzweig, A. (1967). *The hidden order of art*. Los Angeles: University of California Press.

Eigen, M. (1986). *The psychotic core*. Northvale, NJ: Jason Aronson Incorporated.

Freud, S. (1914). Further recommendations in the technique of psychoanalysis. In P. Rieff (Ed.), *Therapy and technique*, 1963. New York: Collier.

Freud, S. (1919). The uncanny. In *On creativity and the unconscious*, 1958. New York: Harper & Row.

Freud, S. (1920). A note on the prehistory of the technique of analysis. In P. Rieff (Ed.), *Therapy and technique*, 1963. New York: Collier.

Freud, S. (1928). Dostoevsky and Parricide SE 21: 177–199, London: Hogarth Press, 1961.

Gendlin, E. T. (1981). *Focusing*. New York: Bantam Books.

Giovacchini, P. (1979). *The treatment of primitive states*. New York: Aronson.

Grotowski, J. (1968). *Towards a poor theatre*. New York: Simon & Schuster.

Grunes, M. (1984). The therapeutic object relationship. *Psychoanalytic Review*, *71*,(1) 123, 143.

Guntrip, H. (1971). *Psychoanalytic theory, therapy and the self*. New York: Basic Books.

Horner, A. (1979). *Object relations and the developing ego in therapy*. New York: Aronson.

Jaffe, J., & Anderson, S. (1979). Communication rhythms and the evolution of language. In A. Siegman & S. Feldstein (Eds.), *Of speech and time: Temporal speech patterns in interpersonal contexts*. Hillsdale, NJ: Lawrence Erlbaum.

Kernberg, O. (1984). *Severe personality disorders: Psychotherapeutic strategies*. New Haven: Yale University Press.

Landy, R. (1983). The use of distancing in drama therapy. *International Journal of Arts in Psychotherapy*, *10*, 175–186.

Landy, R. (1986). *Drama therapy: Concepts and practices*. Springfield: Charles Thomas.

Langer, S. (1953). *Feeling and form*. New York: Charles Scribner's Sons.

Lee, D. (1973). Codifications of reality: Lineal and nonlineal. In R. E. Ornstein (Ed.), *The nature of human consciousness*. San Francisco: W. H. Freeman.

Lichtenberg, J., Bornstein, M., & Silver, D. (Eds.). (1984). *Empathy*. Hillsdale, NJ: Analytic Press.

Loewald, H. W. (1960). On the therapeutic action of psychoanalytic interpretation. *Journal of Psychoanalysis, 41*, 16–33.

Lomax, A. (1982). The cross-cultural variation of rhythmic style. In M. Davis (Ed.), *Interaction rhythms.* New York: Human Sciences Press.

Mann, H., Siegler, M., & Osmond, H. (1972). The psychotypology of time. In H. Yaker, H. Osmond, & F. Cheek (Eds.), *The future of time: Man's temporal environment.* Garden City, NY: Anchor Press, Doubleday.

Moore, S. (1974). *The Stanislavski system.* New York: Viking Press.

Moses, P. J. (1954). *The voice of neurosis.* New York: Grune & Stratton.

The Norton anthology of poetry (1975). New York: W.W. Norton and Co., Inc.

Pirandello, L. (1952). *Naked masks.* New York: Dutton.

Ricoeur, P. (1976). *Interpretation theory: Discourse and the surplus of meaning.* Fort Worth, TX: TCU Press.

Robbins, A. (1981). *Expressive therapy: A creative arts approach to depth-oriented treatment.* New York: Human Sciences Press.

Robbins, A. (1984). Interpretation as a means of organizing psychological space within the transference/countertransference relationship. *Modern Psychoanalysis, 9*, 7–14.

Robbins, A. (1988). *Between therapists: The processing of transference/countertransference material.* New York: Human Sciences Press.

Robbins, A. (1988). The interface of the real and transference relationships in schizoid phenomena. *Psychoanalytic Review, 75*, 393–418.

Rose, B. (Ed.) (1953). *Art as art: The selected writings of Ad Reinhardt.* New York: Viking Press.

Rose, G. (1987). *Trauma and mastery in life and art.* Yale University Press. New Haven: Connecticut.

Rothenberg, A. (1987). *The creative process of psychotherapy.* New York: Norton.

Sartre, J. P. (1942). *Being and nothingness.* New York: Philosophical Library.

Scheff, T. (1979). *Catharsis in healing, ritual, and drama.* Berkeley: University of California Press.

Segal, H. (1973). *Introduction to the work of Melanie Klein.* New York: Basic Books, Inc.

Selected Poems of Rainer Maria Rilke (1981). (R. Bly, Trans.) New York: Harper and Row.

Serlin, I. (1985). Kinaesthetic imagining: A phenomenological study. Unpublished dissertation, University of Dallas.

Shields, A., & Robbins, A. (1980). Music in expressive therapy. In A. Robbins (Ed.), *Expressive therapy: A creative arts approach to depth-oriented treatment.* New York: Human Sciences Press.

Sontag, S. (1961). *Against interpretation.* New York: Dell Books.

Stanislavski, C. (1961). *An actor prepares.* New York: Theatre Arts.

Stern, D. (1985). *The interpersonal world of the infant.* New York: Basic Books.

Stern, A. (1938). Psychoanalytic investigation and therapy in the borderline group of neurosis. *Psychoanalytic Quarterly, 7,* 467–489.

Turner, V. (1969). *The ritual process.* Ithaca, New York: Cornell Paperbacks.

Watkins, M. (1986). *Invisible guests: The development of*

imaginal dialogues. Hillsdale, NJ: The Analytic Press, Lawrence Erlbaum Associates.

Winnicott, D. (1953). Transitional objects and transitional phenomena. *International Journal of Psychoanalysis, 34*, 89–97.

Winnicott, D. W. (1965). *The maturational processes and the facilitating environment*. New York: International Universities Press.

Winnicott, D. W. (1971). *Playing and reality*. New York: Basic Books.

Suggested Reading

Adler, G., & Brue, D. (1979). Aloneness and borderline psychopathology: The possible relevance of child development issues. *International Journal of Psychoanalysis, 60*, 83–96.

Bion, W. R. (1967). *Second thoughts: Selected papers on psychoanalysis*. New York: Basic Books.

Gill, M. (1973). Psychoanalysis and Exploratory Psychotherapy. *Journal of the American Psychoanalytic Association, 21*, 771–79.

Goldstein, W. (1985). *An introduction to the borderline condition*. New Jersey: James Aronson, Inc.

Gunderson, J. (1977). Characteristics of borderlines. In P. Hartocollis (Ed.), *Borderline personality disorders: The concept, the syndrome, the patient*. New York: International University Press.

Huizinga, J. (1950). *Homo Ludens: A study of the play element in culture*. Boston: Beacon Press.

Kandinsky, V. (1977). *Concerning the spiritual in art*. New York: Dover Publications.

Laban, R. (1956). *Principles of dance and movement notation*. London: MacDonald and Evans, Ltd.

Mahler, M. (1968). *On human symbiosis and the vicissitudes of individuation*. New York: International Universities Press.

May, R. (1975). *The courage to create*. New York: Bantam Books.

Masterson, J. (1976). *Psychotherapy of the borderline adult: A developmental approach*. New York: Brunner Mazel.

Masterson, J. (Ed.). (1978). *New perspectives on psychotherapy of the borderline adult*. New York: Brunner Mazel.

Masterson, J. (1981). *The narcissistic and borderline disorders*. New York: Brunner Mazel.

Reinhardt, A. (1953). Art as art: Selected writings. In B. Rose (Ed.), *Documents of 20th century art*. New York: Viking Press.

Robbins, A. (1987). *The artist as therapist*. New York: Human Sciences Press.

Rose, G. (1980). *The power of form*. New York: International Universities Press.

Watkins, M. (1984). *Waking dreams*. Dallas: Spring Publications.

Index

295